The Sunday Cook
C·O·L·L·E·C·T·I·O·N

BY GRACE HOWANIEC

Published by

AMHERST
PRESS

The Sunday Cook
C·O·L·L·E·C·T·I·O·N

First Edition.

Library of Congress Catalog Number 93-70422
ISBN 0-942495-27-6

Also by Grace Howaniec
ENCORE WISCONSIN,
Chefs recipes designed to bring you ovations.
ISBN 0-942495-18-7

This book was printed by
Amherst Press
A division of Palmer Publications, Inc.
P.O. Box 296
Amherst, WI 54406

■ Table of Contents

Dedication

To my family, friends and associates who have graciously shared the best from their tables over the years. This book is a shared joy.

Acknowledgements

To Alan Borsuk, my boss at *Wisconsin* magazine, for the opportunity and privilege of working with the best.

To Paula Brookmire, associate editor at *Wisconsin* who has painstakingly edited each of these recipes. If you find the directions clear and complete, thank Paula. I have, many times.

To Mary Franz, a food stylist who makes the food in my recipes sparkle. Thank you for all your extra effort and care.

To Mike Huibregtse and his talented studio photography staff. Thanks for keeping my image intact.

To Dennis Getto, *Milwaukee Journal* restaurant critic who has shared his expertise with me and enriched my own food experiences.

To Doris Schaffer and Dale Miller, dear friends, who shared their skills in proofing and critiquing this cookbook. Dinner is on me!

To my readers, whose enthusiasm made this book a reality.

To Chuck and Roberta Spanbauer, my publishers at Amherst Press. How lucky can a writer get!

To BJ, again, who has always been a believer.

■ The cover features the Sunday Cook, Grace Howaniec, at home in her kitchen, ready to serve the popular dish, Chicken With 40 Cloves of Garlic. Photo by Huibregtse Studio in Milwaukee, Wisconsin. Cover design by Dunn & Associates Advertising Design in Hayward, Wisconsin. Back cover photo and interior photos by *Milwaukee Journal* photographers. Thank you all for your contribution to *THE SUNDAY COOK*.

Introduction

A phone call from *Wisconsin* magazine editor, Alan Borsuk in the summer of 1990 marked the beginning of this cookbook. Alan was looking for someone to write a weekly food column for the Sunday *Milwaukee Journal* magazine and several staff members had suggested me. "Was I interested?" he asked.

Possibly the way I shrieked "yes" at 100 decibels convinced him that I was, indeed, interested. After subsequent, more subdued interviews I was hired to write the column which we named *The Sunday Cook*. Alan promised me that he would make me "rich and famous." I promised that I would meet my deadlines and not, knowingly, poison anyone.

I chose recipes that were personal favorites of mine, family or friends. Sometimes I chose a promising recipe from a new cookbook that I reviewed. In between, I sandwiched some Wisconsin chef's recipes or cooking school owner's specialties that featured food on the cutting edge of the culinary scene. And when I traveled anywhere, whatever I tasted, I considered it as a potential feature.

The Sunday Cook column was launched with a bread pudding recipe from California and moved rapidly to my mother's famous Peanut Brittle, my Aunt Marie's molded Christmas salad, Jill Prescott's Chocolate Truffle Raspberry Cheesecake and Chicken With 40 Cloves of Garlic.

Reaction to the column was respectful and reserved until Chicken With 40 Cloves of Garlic was published in February 1991. It rattled cages and raised a rukus. Letters and phone calls flooded the office. Most were ecstatic, "my house had a lovely aroma of thyme, sage and rosemary," "my husband says it is delicious," "I will make this again," "this is a keeper."

One letterwriter, however, was a bit less enthusiastic. She said it would take until spring for her house to lose the pungent garlic aroma. When the *Wisconsin* "Dialogue" column published that letter, follow-up letters defended the recipe and questioned the complaining cook's techniques. Suddenly we had controversy, the lifeblood of any column—and a following.

From that point on, *The Sunday Cook* settled in comfortably with its readership. I knew that the recipes were finding their fans when on a Sunday morning, a fellow parishioner greeted me not with the communal sign of peace but with, "I just loved your Salted Peanut Crunchies!"

People began saving the columns—stuffing them into kitchen drawers and sometimes loaning them out and not getting them back. Requests for reprints came to me and to the *Wisconsin* office. "Are you ever going to put those recipes together in a book," readers asked. "Help—I'm running out of drawer space."

And so *The Sunday Cook Collection* was born. I have attempted to include every recipe that especially pleased readers. Chefs, cooking schools owners and teachers and most publishers were delighted to have their work included. I want to thank them for the generous sharing of their gifts. Several column favorites are not included because I couldn't obtain permission to reprint. Most notably, the recipe for "Jerk Chicken" is missing. If you still have that clipping from *Wisconsin*, put it among the pages of this cookbook and guard it well.

(If you have lost a favorite recipe from the column and it is not printed in this collection, send a *self-addressed, stamped envelope* with the names of the recipe(s) needed to: *Wisconsin* Magazine, Milwaukee Journal, PO Box 661, Milwaukee, Wisconsin 53201.)

My publishers, Chuck and Roberta Spanbauer of Amherst Press and I decided we wanted to include some of the glorious food photos taken by Milwaukee Journal photographers for the magazine food features. They are included on the back cover and on the inside pages of the book. We thank the *Journal* and its talented photographers for making this addition possible.

This second cookbook, *The Sunday Cook Collection*, joins my first cookbook, *Encore Wisconsin*, in presenting the culinary riches of a state which I have come to treasure for the pleasures of its tables—and the friendships forged there.

The Sunday Cook

C·O·L·L·E·C·T·I·O·N

■ Breads, Brunch and Such

Banana chocolate chip pecan bread

1 cup sugar
1 large egg
½ cup unsalted butter, softened
1 cup mashed ripe banana (about 2 large bananas)*
3 tablespoons milk
2 cups flour
1 teaspoon baking powder
½ teaspoon baking soda
1 cup semisweet chocolate chips
½ cup chopped pecans

*B*anana breads used to be boring fare to me. They all tasted pretty much the same. Then the owners of Water's Edge Resort in Birchwood, Betty and Milt Jantzen, pressed a tiny loaf of this ethereal snack into my hands as we were leaving their guest cottage. It was love at first bite. Do try this tasty bread.

From The Elsah Landing Restaurant Cookbook, *PO Box 99, Elsah, Illinois 62028. Reprinted with permission.*

In large mixing bowl, cream sugar, egg and butter with electric mixer until mixture is fluffy, about 3 minutes; set aside. In small bowl, mix bananas and milk; set aside.

Sift together flour, baking powder and baking soda onto paper plate. Add dry ingredients to creamed butter mixture alternately with banana mixture, stirring together with rubber spatula until dry ingredients are blended, about 1 minute. Stir in chocolate chips and pecans.

Spoon batter into a 9¼-by-5¼-by-2¾-inch greased and floured loaf pan. Drop pan twice, from height of 6 inches to counter, to remove any air bubbles. Bake in preheated, 350-degree oven 1 hour, or until wooden toothpick inserted in center of crack comes out clean. Cool in pan on wire rack 10 minutes. Remove bread to wire rack to complete cooling.

Makes 1 loaf.

*Note: The riper the bananas, the more flavorful the bread.

Photo on page 46

Pumpkin-cranberry nut bread

3½ **cups flour**
2 **teaspoons ground cinnamon**
1 **teaspoon salt**
1 **teaspoon baking soda**
½ **teaspoon baking powder**
2 **teaspoons grated orange zest**
¾ **cup low-calorie margarine,
    softened***
1½ **cups sugar**
3 **large eggs**
1 **can (16 ounces) solid-pack
    pumpkin**
1 **cup chopped walnuts**
1 **cup fresh or frozen
    cranberries (unthawed)**

This reduced-fat pumpkin bread uses low-calorie margarine and whole fresh or frozen cranberries for color and pizazz. Keep this recipe in mind when fall harvest brings in a surfeit of pumpkins and cranberries.

In large bowl, mix flour, cinnamon, salt, baking soda, baking powder and orange zest (outer peel of orange) with wire whisk until blended; set aside.

In another large mixing bowl, use an electric mixer to cream margarine and sugar, scraping down sides of bowl with rubber spatula after 1½ minutes of mixing. Continue beating until light and fluffy, another 1½ minutes. Add eggs, one at a time; beating 1 minute after each addition. Add pumpkin and reserved flour mixture alternately, stirring with spatula until just blended. Gently stir in walnuts and cranberries. (If cranberries are fresh, you may choose to cut them in half. If frozen, add them whole to batter.)

Spoon batter into 2 lightly greased, 9-by-5-by-3-inch loaf baking pans. Smooth out surfaces with spatula. Drop both pans from a height of 6 inches to counter to remove air bubbles. Bake in a preheated, 350-degree oven 60 to 65 minutes, or until breads test done when toothpick inserted in center comes out clean. Cool in pans on rack 10 minutes; remove from pans to rack to cool completely.

Makes 2 loaves.

***Note:** I use Fleischmann's Light Corn-Oil Spread, which has 33 percent less fat, salt and calories than regular margarine.

Irish soda bread

2 cups flour
2 tablespoons brown sugar
1½ teaspoons baking powder
½ teaspoon baking soda
½ teaspoon salt
2 tablespoons unsalted butter
¾ cup plus 2 tablespoons buttermilk, at room temperature
½ cup golden raisins or currants

My mother-in-law helped me track down a recipe that came close to the scrumptious Irish Soda Bread sold in her South Side Chicago ethnic neighborhood bakery. Brown sugar, buttermilk and golden raisins make the difference in this bread that is heavenly, sliced fresh, and out-of-this-world, toasted.

In medium-sized bowl, combine flour, sugar, baking powder, baking soda and salt with wire whisk, stirring just to blend. Cut in butter with pastry cutter until mixture has texture of cornmeal. Stir in buttermilk and mix thoroughly into a soft dough. Add raisins or currants, incorporating into dough.

Turn dough out on lightly floured surface and knead gently until smooth, about 3 minutes. Form dough into 7-inch-diameter flattened round loaf and place in lightly oiled 9-inch-round, 2-inch-deep cake pan.

With kitchen shears or sharp knife, cut a cross shape about ½ inch deep in center of round of dough. Bake at 375 degrees about 40 minutes, until a medium golden brown. Remove from pan; place flat side down on wire rack and let cool at least an hour. To store bread, wrap with foil or plastic.

Makes 1 loaf.

Audrey's yeast butterhorns

2 cups milk
½ cup unsalted butter plus
   melted butter for brushing
   over rolls (divided)
2 packages (¼ ounce each)
   quick-rise yeast
¾ cup sugar
2 large eggs
2 teaspoons salt
6½ to 7 cups flour

4-H kids (no matter their ages) all recognize yeast butterhorns, a staple in county and state fair baking competitions. This prize-winning recipe comes from Audrey Hopkins of Oconomowoc who won the purple grand champion ribbon at the Waukesha County Fair for these tender and airy classic yeast rolls.

Heat milk in saucepan or in microwaveable bowl to 180 degrees (scalding). Remove from heat; transfer to large mixing bowl. Add butter, stirring until butter melts, about 3 minutes. Cool mixture to lukewarm (110 to 115 degrees); add dry yeast and mix well until dissolved.

Add sugar, eggs, salt and 3 cups of the flour. Beat well, using dough-hook attachment or beaters on medium speed, about 3 minutes, or until smooth. Add remaining flour; beat another 4 minutes. (Mixture will be a little sticky.)

Cover bowl with clean linen towel and let stand until doubled in volume, about 1½ hours. Then divide dough into 3 even portions. Place each dough portion in center of lightly floured surface. With hands, form each into a 6-inch round. With lightly floured rolling pin, roll out each round from center to outer edges until it's ¼-inch thick. Using sharp knife, cut dough circle into 4 pie-shaped quarters; cut each quarter into pie-shaped thirds.

Roll up each wedge beginning at wide edge and ending at point. Place wedges, point-sides-down, on greased cookie sheet, 3 inches apart. Let rise, covered with clean towel, until doubled in volume, 1 to 1½ hours. To test if dough has risen sufficiently, gently press fingertip into dough. Finger imprint will remain when dough is ready.

Bake at 350 degrees in preheated oven 12 to 14 minutes, or until a light golden brown. Remove to wire rack to complete cooling. Brush surfaces with additional melted butter, if desired.

Makes 36 rolls.

Cheese-yeast rolls

- 1 package (¼ ounce) quick-rising active dry yeast
- 1 cup warm water (110 to 115 degrees)
- 2 teaspoons honey (divided)
- 2 cups white flour
- 1 cup whole-wheat flour
- 1 can (15 ounces) cooked garbanzo beans, drained (about 1½ cups)
- ¾ cup grated sharp Cheddar cheese
- 1 teaspoon ground cumin
- 1¼ teaspoons salt
- 4 to 5 tablespoons olive oil (divided)

When a state fair judge with the credentials of Rosalie Powell tells you to pay attention to a particular recipe, I give that recipe priority. These award-winning cheese-yeast rolls won a first place prize in 1991 for veteran food contestant, Joan Gaska of West Allis. They are pretty, nutritious and intriguing in flavors. Serve them with a vegetarian chili for maximum nutrition and complementary flavors.

In small bowl, dissolve yeast in warm water and ½ teaspoon of the honey. Let stand 5 minutes, until small bubbles form on surface. (If yeast does not bubble, discard and start with new yeast.) Transfer yeast mixture to large mixing bowl of heavy-duty mixer. Add white and whole-wheat flours, blending well with mixer about 2 minutes.

Mash beans well in blender or food processor or by hand with a fork. Add beans, cheese, cumin, salt, remaining 1½ teaspoons honey and 1 tablespoon of the olive oil to dough in bowl, mixing to blend. Add more whole-wheat flour if needed until dough is no longer sticky.

Knead dough by hand or with a heavy-duty mixer with dough hook until smooth, about 3 minutes with dough hook or 6 minutes by hand. Put dough in greased bowl and cover with clean towel. Let rise in warm place (75 to 80 degrees) until doubled in volume, about 45 minutes with quick-rising yeast (1½ hours if you use regular yeast). Punch dough down with hands. Remove dough to floured surface; knead 2 to 3 minutes by hand, pushing dough away from you with heels of hands, turning dough over and repeating motion.

When dough is smooth and elastic, shape into sixteen, 2½-inch-diameter round rolls. Place 1½ inches apart on greased baking sheets. Use sharp knife to make 3 parallel slashes in top of each roll. Let rise in warm place until doubled in volume, about 30 minutes for quick yeast (1 hour for regular yeast).

Bake at 350 degrees 10 minutes. Brush with part of remaining olive oil. Bake 10 minutes more until golden brown, a total of 20 minutes. Remove from oven to wire rack. Brush immediately with remaining olive oil. Cool completely. Store, tightly covered, at room temperature or freeze.

Makes 16 rolls.

Lemon scones

4½ cups biscuit mix
¼ cup brown sugar
1 cup currants or golden raisins
1 tablespoon grated lemon zest
(zest of 1 large lemon)
1 large whole egg, beaten,
at room temperature
1 cup milk, room temperature
1 egg white
1 teaspoon water
Raw sugar or granulated
sugar
Unsalted butter

I'm a sucker for anything lemon-flavored and my family and friends know my inherent weakness. My sister, Judy Amfahr, shared this favorite tea scone recipe with me one summer and I've been baking them ever since. The recipe uses packaged biscuit mix for ease of preparation.

In large mixing bowl, blend biscuit mix and brown sugar with wire whisk; stir in currants and lemon zest; set aside.

In small bowl, mix whole egg and milk; add to dry ingredients, stirring only until flour is moistened. Turn out on floured surface. Dust with flour. Pat dough or gently roll with rolling pin to ½-inch thickness. Cut scones with floured 2½-inch biscuit cutter, dipping cutter in flour after each cut.

Place scones 2 inches apart on greased baking sheet. Brush off any excess flour from top of scones. Combine egg white with water. Brush mixture over top of scones; sprinkle with raw sugar.

Bake at 400 degrees for 10 to 12 minutes, until golden brown. Serve warm with unsalted butter.

Makes about 20 scones.

Apricot-hazelnut coffeecake

1 package (6 ounces) dried
  apricots
1½ cups flour plus 3
  tablespoons (divided)
½ cup granulated sugar
1 tablespoon baking powder
¼ teaspoon salt
¼ teaspoon ground mace
6 tablespoons softened butter
  (divided)
1 large egg
½ cup milk
⅓ cup brown sugar
½ teaspoon ground cinnamon
⅓ cup chopped hazelnuts or
  walnuts

Apricot-anything gets high marks from me. I love apricots fresh baked in cream and sprinkled with vanilla sugar, or dried and used in all manner of breads and stuffings. This coffeecake pairs hazelnuts (filberts) and apricots in a grand quick coffeecake for brunch. Serve it with Canadian Bacon or baked ham.

Rinse apricots with warm water, place in 2-quart saucepan and cover with 1½ cups water. Bring to boil over medium-high heat, then boil gently 10 minutes. Drain off water; discard. Let apricots cool on chopping board.

Reserve 9 apricot halves for topping; dice remaining into ¼-inch pieces; set aside.

In medium mixing bowl, whisk together 1½ cups of the flour, white sugar, baking powder, salt and mace; cut in 4 tablespoons of the butter with pastry blender until mixture looks like cornmeal.

In small bowl, mix together egg and milk; add to dry ingredients, blending well. Add chopped apricots and blend. Spread batter evenly in 9-inch-square, greased glass baking dish. Arrange reserved 9 apricot halves over top.

Make topping in small bowl by mixing brown sugar, cinnamon, remaining 3 tablespoons flour, remaining 2 tablespoons butter and nuts. Sprinkle topping over coffeecake. Bake in preheated 350-degree oven 35 to 40 minutes, or until cake tests done when wooden pick is inserted in center. Serve warm.

Makes 9 servings.

Whole-wheat sourdough waffles

1 cup unbleached all-purpose
flour
1 cup whole-wheat pastry
flour*
2 cups lukewarm milk
½ cup sourdough potato
starter
2 tablespoons sugar
½ teaspoon salt
½ teaspoon baking powder
5 tablespoons melted butter
or margarine
3 eggs*
½ teaspoon baking soda,
dissolved in 1 tablespoon
water

Overnight potato starter

2 large baking potatoes, peeled
4 cups water (divided)
1 package (¼ ounce) active dry
yeast
1 tablespoon white corn syrup
2 teaspoons salt
2 cups flour

*S*ourdough fans are always looking
for new ways to use up their
treasured starter. Try these part
whole-wheat pancakes that are leav-
ened with a quick (overnight) starter
made from potatoes and yeast. I like to
serve these with maple syrup or apple
syrup spiked with cinnamon. They are
incredibly light and pleasurable to eat.

Beat flours, milk and potato starter in large
mixing bowl with wire whisk until smooth, 1
to 2 minutes. Let stand in warm place overnight, covered with waxed paper.

Next morning, beat down waffle batter and
add sugar, salt, baking powder and melted
butter. Beat in eggs. Gently fold in baking
soda-water mixture. Batter will be pourable,
not thick. Preheat waffle iron on high until
light goes out (it reaches high temperature).
Grease iron lightly with vegetable oil. Use
½ cup batter for each waffle in a 7-inch-
diameter waffle iron. Pour batter onto iron,
close iron and cook about 4 minutes on high
(or follow manufacturer's directions on your
iron).

Makes 8 to 10 seven-inch-diameter waffles
(or 4 servings of about 2 waffles each).

*Notes: Whole-wheat pastry flour, which
has a finer texture than regular flour, can be
purchased at health-food stores and some
supermarkets. Instead of 3 eggs, you can use
1 egg plus 2 egg whites, for less cholesterol.

Overnight potato starter

Cut potatoes into 1-inch chunks to make
about 2 cups. In medium saucepan, cook
potatoes, covered, in about 3½ cups of the
water over medium heat until tender, about
15 minutes. Mash potatoes and potato liquid
together in large glass bowl. Cool to room
temperature.

Heat remaining ½ cup water to 110 to 115 degrees, put in small bowl, add yeast and dissolve in warm water; add to potato mixture. Add syrup and salt; gradually add flour, stirring until smooth.

Cover loosely and let stand in warm place (or in refrigerator) overnight or until bubbly; starter should have a distinct sour aroma. Stir before using.

Note: Ideally, you should subtract 1 cup of starter each week (either to use in a recipe or to discard). Each time, replenish, or "feed," the starter with ¾ cup warm water and ¾ cup flour. Let stand, loosely covered, overnight. Stir down. Cover and store in refrigerator. If you forget about the starter for 3 or 4 weeks, discard half of mixture and replenish with 2 cups warm water and 2 cups flour. Let stand, loosely covered, overnight. Stir down. Cover and store in refrigerator. Starter will separate when stored; this is normal; simply stir down to blend.

The life or bubbliness of starter depends on its storage. Some starters have been passed from one generation to another; some last a few days. When you replenish starter, pour it into a freshly cleaned but dry container. If starter darkens significantly from its normal yellowish-white color, discard.

Stuffed Grand Marnier French toast

12 slices quality, firm-textured white bread*
1 stick butter or margarine
1 package (8 ounces) cream cheese, softened
4 tablespoons Grand Marnier or orange juice (divided)
1½ teaspoons grated orange zest
½ cup chopped pecans (optional)
8 eggs or equivalent amount of egg substitute*
2½ cups milk
2 tablespoons granulated sugar
Strawberry or maple syrup
Powdered sugar (optional)

Make-ahead brunch dishes are cooks' favorites when entertaining overnight guests. Try this lovely stuffed French Toast recipe infused with orange flavors the next time family or friends stay over. You can use an egg substitute, if you want to reduce fat. I would serve this with a strawberry-flavored syrup.

Butter 1 side of each bread slice; lay 6 slices flat, buttered side down, in lightly buttered 13-by-9-by-3-inch pan.

In small bowl, mix cream cheese, 2 tablespoons of the Grand Marnier, orange zest and pecans, if desired; spread evenly over bread in pan. Place remaining bread slices over top, buttered side up.

In medium bowl, beat eggs, milk, granulated sugar and remaining 2 tablespoons Grand Marnier until well-blended. Pour over bread slices in pan. Refrigerate overnight.

An hour before you're ready to serve brunch, bake bread at 350 degrees 50 minutes. Serve hot with syrup. Dust with powdered sugar, if desired.

Makes 6 to 8 servings.

*Notes: Pepperidge Farm Toasting (thick-sliced) white bread is excellent, as is Brownberry Ovens white bread. I prefer either the Second Nature or Egg Supreme brands of egg substitute.

Swedish cardamom pancakes

3 large eggs
1 teaspoon granulated sugar
½ teaspoon salt
⅛ teaspoon freshly ground
   cardamom seed
1 cup milk (divided)
½ cup flour
10 tablespoons unsalted butter
   (divided)
1 cup fresh or frozen
   cranberries, partially thawed
1 cup powdered sugar
1 tablespoon freshly squeezed
   lemon juice, strained
   Fresh cranberry butter
   or Lingonberry jam

My German-Tyrolean grandfather made his mother's version of Tyrolean pancakes for us whenever he came to make sausage on our Iowa farm. I loved his egg-rich thin pancakes and tried to duplicate them for my children when they were young. My best attempt came from a church cookbook with a recipe for Swedish pancakes. When my grown children are home, they still ask for these thin and tender pancakes. I share them in the same spirit of love and fellowship that my Grandpa Klocker shared them with his grandchildren.

In blender, mix eggs until blended. Add granulated sugar, salt, cardamom seed and ½ cup of the milk. Blend thoroughly. Stir in flour, remaining ½ cup milk and 2 tablespoons of butter that has been melted; blend to mix. Pour batter into 2-cup glass measure; set aside.

To make cranberry butter, rinse out blender (or use food processor) and puree cranberries until nearly smooth. Add powdered sugar, remaining 8 tablespoons of unmelted butter and lemon juice. Blend or process until smooth. Refrigerate.

Heat a 10-inch-diameter, non-stick skillet over medium-high heat. Brush surface lightly with additional unsalted butter. Using 3 tablespoons batter per pancake, pour batter into skillet, tilting skillet to spread batter evenly to cover skillet bottom. Cook 30 seconds, or until bottom of pancake is a mottled golden brown. Loosen edges of pancake carefully with wooden spatula; flip and cook about 30 seconds more, until bottom is golden brown. Pancakes are thin and fragile; so handle carefully. Remove to heated platter; repeat until all batter is cooked.

To eat, spread pancakes with cranberry butter or lingonberry jam. Roll up, side by side, with lapped edge of the roll touching bottom of platter.

Makes ten 10-inch-diameter pancakes.

Strawberry blintzes

- 2 ounces cream cheese
- 1 egg yolk
- 1 teaspoon vanilla extract
- 1 tablespoon lemon juice
- 1 teaspoon grated lemon zest
- ¼ cup sugar
- 1 cup small-curd cottage cheese
- ¼ cup ricotta cheese
- 4 cups fresh strawberries, cleaned, stemmed (divided)
- 1 cup unbleached flour*
- 4 large eggs
- ¼ cup melted, unsalted butter plus butter for greasing
- ½ teaspoon salt
- 1¾ cups milk
- Sour cream (optional)

You can buy ready-made frozen or refrigerated crepes in specialty stores or make these tender French pancakes from scratch using a recipe I adapted from Janet Ballantyne's cookbook, The Joy of Gardening†. This is a special occasion breakfast or brunch dish, preferably prepared when strawberries are in season. (Remember you can make crepes in advance and freeze them for later serving ease.)

†Reprinted by permission from GARDEN WAY, INC. Copyright © 1984, GARDEN WAY, INC. All rights reserved.

Start by making blintz filling: Add cream cheese, egg yolk, vanilla, lemon juice and zest, and sugar to bowl of food processor; process 30 seconds, until well-blended. (Or mix by hand in mixing bowl about 2 minutes.) Add cottage cheese and ricotta. Using pulsing button on processor, process for 3 short pulses. (Or mix in by hand till well-blended.) Chop 1 cup of the strawberries into ¼-inch pieces; fold into cheese mixture. Cover and refrigerate filling until ready to use.

Make thin pancakes* by mixing flour, eggs, melted butter, salt and milk in food processor or blender until smooth, about 30 seconds. Batter should have consistency of half-and-half; add more milk if necessary. Refrigerate 1 hour to allow flour to absorb liquid for a tender crepe.

Heat 6-inch-diameter, non-stick skillet over medium heat and brush lightly with butter to cover bottom and up ½ inch on sides of skillet. Pour 3 tablespoons of batter into center of pan; quickly tip pan, moving it in a circular fashion to cover bottom of pan. Cook 2 minutes, until underside is speckled brown and top of pancake looks firm; turn and cook 30 seconds more. Repeat with rest of batter.

Arrange cooked pancakes in 1 layer on wire rack so they will cool and dry, at least 5 minutes. Recipe makes about 20 pancakes, 5½ inches in diameter. You'll need only 12 for the blintzes, but some early attempts may have to be discarded. The extra pancakes can be stacked, wrapped in foil, placed in a plastic bag and frozen.

When 12 pancakes are dry, spoon ¼ cup strawberry-cheese mixture into center of each. Fold up bottom third of pancake to cover filling, then fold in sides (like an envelope). Finally, fold top third of crepe down to seal (like a burrito). Place 12 filled blintzes seam-side-down in lightly buttered, 13-by-9-by-2-inch baking dish; cover with foil; bake in preheated, 350 degree oven 25 minutes, or until blintzes are hot.

While blintzes bake, slice remaining 3 cups strawberries. Remove blintzes from oven spread with sliced strawberries and serve at once with dollops of sour cream, if desired.

Makes 12 blintzes.

*Notes: Wondra or instant-blending flour also may be used. If you don't want to make pancakes, you can buy ready-made pancakes or crepes in frozen or refrigerated sections of specialty groceries.

Irresistible winter compote

1¾ cups apple juice
¼ cup cranberry juice
½ cup pitted prunes
½ cup dried apricots
¼ cup raisins
¼ cup bourbon (optional)*
4 thin slices fresh lemon
¼ teaspoon ground ginger
2 sticks cinnamon
1 tart apple
1 pear
¼ cup sugar
1 can (11 ounces) mandarin
    orange sections, drained
1 jar (6 ounces) maraschino
    cherries, drained (optional)*
1 tablespoon Grand Marnier
    (optional)*
Granola
Star fruit for garnish
    (optional)

*S*erve this colorful compote from the Ridgeway House in La Conner, Washington with your next brunch. The combination of fresh, dried and canned fruits makes this compote feasible especially in winter.

From Breakfast in Bed—The Best B & B Recipes from Northern California to British Columbia *by Carol Friebery. Copyright © 1990. Reprinted with permission of Sasquatch Books, Seattle.*

In a large, heavy saucepan, bring juices, prunes, apricots and raisins to a boil. Add bourbon, if desired, lemon slices, ginger and stick cinnamon. Reduce heat to low, cover and simmer 15 minutes.

Meanwhile, peel, core and cut both apple and pear into thin wedges; add with sugar to dried fruits that have simmered 15 minutes; simmer mixture 5 to 7 minutes more, until fruit is tender. Add mandarin orange sections, cherries and liqueur, if desired; remove from heat. Remove lemon slices and cinnamon sticks and discard.

Spoon compote into individual dishes. Sprinkle with granola and garnish with star fruit, if desired. Can be served warm or cool.

Makes 6 servings.

*Notes: Orange juice may be substituted for bourbon and liqueur. And dried red fruits such as cherries or dried cranberries can be added to the dried fruit mixture instead of maraschino cherries.

Wine Country Inn granola

3 cups old-fashioned oats
1 cup slivered or sliced
    almonds
¼ cup butter, melted
¼ cup brown sugar
¼ cup honey
¼ teaspoon ground cinnamon
1 cup flaked coconut
1 cup golden raisins

Our favorite place to stay in California's Napa Valley is the Wine Country Inn just outside of St. Helena where this marvelous granola is a breakfast staple. The owners graciously share their recipe with guests. It is special enough for company-brunch.

Mix together oats and almonds in 15-by-10-by-1-inch jelly roll pan; set aside. In small bowl, mix butter, brown sugar and honey. Pour over oats, stirring well to combine. Sprinkle with cinnamon; stir to mix. Spread mixture evenly in pan.

Bake, uncovered, at 250 degrees 30 to 35 minutes, or until light brown. Remove from oven; stir in coconut and bake about 45 minutes more, until golden brown, stirring regularly every 15 minutes. Remove from oven; stir in raisins.

Let cool in pan on cooling rack; when cool, transfer to tightly covered containers and store at room temperature.

Makes 7 one-cup servings.

Note: This recipe may be doubled, pan size permitting; add 15 minutes to baking time.

Polenta triangles

6½ cups water
1 tablespoon salt ½ teaspoon (divided)
2 cups coarsely ground yellow cornmeal*
1 stick unsalted butter, cut in tablespoons
½ cup freshly grated Parmesan cheese
1½ pounds fresh ripe tomatoes
1 shallot, finely chopped
2 garlic cloves, minced
6 tablespoons olive oil (divided)
¼ teaspoon freshly ground black pepper
1 teaspoon minced fresh rosemary or basil (optional)

*T*ra Vigne Ristorante in St. Helena, California served these crisp polenta triangles with Osso Bucco during a fall visit to Napa Valley. They reminded me of my mother's fried corn meal mush which I always loved. This polenta has the added richness of Parmesan cheese and makes a great side dish instead of potatoes, pasta or rice. I love these with anything tomato flavored.

In heavy 3-quart saucepan, bring water to boil. Stir in one tablespoon salt, reduce heat so that water simmers. Very slowly add cornmeal in thin stream while stirring with wooden spoon. When all cornmeal has been added, lower heat slightly until cornmeal is just barely bubbling. Continue cooking, stirring constantly, until mixture is thick and smooth and comes away from sides of pan, about 25 minutes.

Remove from heat and stir in butter pieces and Parmesan until well-blended. Spoon into well-buttered, 13-by-9-by-2-inch glass baking dish. Smooth top with spatula. Cover with plastic wrap and set in refrigerator to chill and set, at least 3 hours.

Make tomato coulis by plunging tomatoes into boiling water 20 to 30 seconds, until skins burst or slip easily from tomatoes; cut off tops and seed, squeezing tomato gently to remove seeds.

Chop tomatoes in half-inch cubes and add with shallot and garlic to work bowl of food processor or blender. Blend on high speed 10 seconds. Slowly pour in 2 tablespoons of the olive oil while continuing to pulse.

Pour tomato coulis into small saucepan; bring to boil over medium-high heat; reduce heat to simmer for 1 minute. Add ½ teaspoon salt and ¼ teaspoon freshly ground pepper. Return to blender or processor and add 1 teaspoon fresh rosemary, if desired. Process 30 seconds.

Cut chilled polenta into approximately 3-inch squares; then cut each square diagonally into two triangles. Brush a heavy cast-iron skillet with 1 to 2 tablespoons of olive oil; drizzle remaining oil over tops of triangles. Place triangles in skillet in preheated 500-degree oven. Bake 10 minutes; turn triangles over. Bake 10 minutes more. Pour ¼ cup warm tomato coulis onto salad plates; place baked polenta triangles in center of coulis. Serve immediately.

Makes about 12 servings.

*Note: Coarsely ground cornmeal can be found at Italian markets.

Deviled eggs divan

1 pound fresh broccoli florets, washed

10 hard-cooked eggs, peeled and halved lengthwise

2 ounces deviled ham (¼ cup) or 2 ounces ground ham

½ teaspoon Worcestershire sauce

1 teaspoon grated onion

1 tablespoon prepared (liquid) mustard

⅛ teaspoon cayenne pepper

1 tablespoon cream or evaporated milk

1 tablespoon mayonnaise

1 teaspoon salt (divided)

10 tablespoons butter or margarine (divided)

6 tablespoons flour

3 cups milk

2 cups grated sharp Cheddar cheese

¼ teaspoon dry mustard
Dash of freshly ground black pepper

1 cup soft bread crumbs
Paprika for garnish

Good friend, good cook, Betsy Michael, served this recipe to a gathering of our women writing friends during one of our treasured yearly reunions. This brunch dish can be assembled in advance and refrigerated until time of baking. It is delicious with a subtly-spiced sweet yeast bread.

Trim broccoli, cut in 2-inch lengths and place, undrained, in 13-by-9-by-2-inch glass baking dish; cover with plastic wrap and microwave on high 2 minutes. Drain off any moisture. Set aside.

Remove yolks from egg halves and mash on flat plate with ham, Worcestershire sauce, onion, prepared mustard, cayenne pepper, cream, mayonnaise and ¼ teaspoon of the salt. Use to refill egg-white halves, dividing deviled-yolk mixture evenly among egg whites. Set aside.

Make cheese sauce by melting 6 tablespoons of the butter in heavy, medium-sized saucepan over medium heat. Stir in flour with wire whisk and cook 1 minute. Remove pan from heat and gradually whisk in milk. Return to heat and whisk constantly until mixture boils. Boil 1 minute.

Stir in cheese, dry mustard, remaining ¾ teaspoon salt and ground black pepper to taste. Cook, stirring constantly, until cheese melts and mixture is smooth.

Nestle filled egg-white halves around and over top of broccoli; pour cheese sauce over all.

Mix soft bread crumbs and remaining 4 tablespoons of melted butter; sprinkle evenly over eggs. Dust with paprika for garnish.

Bake at 375 degrees 25 minutes, or until sauce bubbles and broccoli is fork-tender.

Makes about 10 servings.

The Sunday Cook
C·O·L·L·E·C·T·I·O·N

 Appetizers

Guacamole-shrimp tortilla chips

1 pound medium shrimp (about 25)
2 ripe avocados
1 teaspoon salt
2½ tablespoons fresh lemon juice
1 clove garlic, minced
2 tablespoons chopped scallions
Dash of chili powder
Dash of cayenne pepper
50 round tortilla chips
50 cilantro leaves or flat-leaf parsley for garnish

*S*hrimp appetizers are favorites for any occasion. Consider this pretty, combination finger food from the award-winning Gatherings-A Collection of Highly Entertaining Menus† *by the Junior League of Milwaukee. Build this appetizer beginning with round crisp corn chips, topped with a spicy homemade guacamole and then decorated with half a shrimp and a sprig of cilantro or flat-leaf parsley.*

†From Gatherings-A Collection of Highly Entertaining Menus, *edited by F. Lynn Nelson, Junior League of Milwaukee.*

Place shrimp over boiling water in vegetable steamer, cover and steam 3 to 5 minutes, until shrimp turn from translucent to opaque white; rinse under cold water 1 to 2 minutes. Peel shrimp, devein and cut each shrimp in half; chill thoroughly in refrigerator in covered container.

Peel and pit avocados and mash avocado meat with fork on flat plate. Add salt, lemon juice, garlic, scallions, chili powder and cayenne pepper; mix well. Cover guacamole tightly with plastic wrap until about 15 minutes before serving time. Spread tortilla chips with guacamole and top with shrimp halves. Garnish with cilantro leaves.

Makes 50 appetizers (plan on 3 to 6 per person).

Fresca salsa

2 pounds fresh tomatoes,
  washed
4 scallions, washed, finely
  chopped
2 cans (4 ounces each) diced
  green chilies
2 cans (4 ounces each)
  chopped black olives
3 tablespoons vegetable or
  olive oil
1 tablespoon red wine vinegar
¼ teaspoon ground cumin
¼ teaspoon crumbled leaf
  oregano
¼ teaspoon salt
¼ teaspoon freshly ground
  black pepper
1 to 2 tablespoons freshly
  minced cilantro
  Corn chips

Lighter, more healthful appetizers are very much in vogue and freshly made salsas sporting vegetables and sometimes fruits are definitely mainstream starters. Fresh or canned chili peppers add a bit of heat but neither of these are fire starters. Serve the tomato-based fresca salsa with crisp corn chips or tortillas; the nectarine salsa with grilled chicken, turkey or pork.

Drain tomatoes and cut off tops; squeeze tomatoes to remove seeds. Dice tomatoes into ¼-inch pieces (should yield about 4 cups). Place in large mixing bowl. Add scallions, green chilies and olives. Fold together to blend; set aside.

In small bowl or jar, whisk together oil, vinegar, cumin, oregano, salt and pepper. Pour over tomato mixture; fold gently to blend. Cover and refrigerate.

Before serving, sprinkle minced cilantro over salsa; stir to blend. Serve chilled with fresh corn chips. Use within 48 hours for best flavors and texture. Refrigerate leftovers.

Makes 6 cups salsa.

Nectarine salsa

2 cups washed, diced
  nectarines
⅓ cup diced red bell pepper
1 tablespoon fresh lime juice
2 teaspoons vegetable oil
1 teaspoon minced fresh
  cilantro
1 teaspoon minced jalapeno
  pepper*

Unpeeled nectarines and bell pepper that have been diced into ¼-inch pieces should be mixed in medium-size bowl. In small bowl, mix lime juice, oil, cilantro and jalapeno; whisk to blend. Pour over nectarine mixture, stirring to blend. Refrigerate, covered. Serve chilled with grilled chicken, turkey or pork.

Makes 4 servings.

*Note: Use caution when using hot chili peppers . . . wear kitchen gloves when handling and rinse hands thoroughly with cold water when finished.

Liver-peppercorn pâté

6 tablespoons unsalted butter
½ cup finely minced onion
2 cloves garlic, peeled and chopped
1 teaspoon dried leaf thyme
½ cup celery tops
10 black peppercorns
2 bay leaves
1 pound chicken livers
2 tablespoons cognac
½ teaspoon salt
½ teaspoon ground allspice
5 teaspoons water-packed green peppercorns, drained (divided)
¼ cup heavy cream

*S*ome *of my best recipes come from friends who share their favorite recipes with me. Mary Meinz has treated me to some wonderful foods and recipes over the years. Try both her pâté and spiced pecans. Be advised, the pecans have some "heat" to them but are great with cocktails or wine.*

In 10-inch skillet, melt butter. Add onion, garlic and thyme and cook, covered, over medium heat about 10 minutes, or until onion is tender and lightly colored.

Meanwhile, in medium saucepan filled with 6 cups water, add celery tops, black peppercorns and bay leaves; bring to boil, reduce heat and simmer about 10 minutes; add chicken livers and simmer gently another 10 minutes; livers should still be slightly pink inside. Drain; discard celery, bay leaves and peppercorns.

Place cooked livers and onion mixture in bowl of food processor fitted with steel blade. Add cognac, salt, allspice and 4 teaspoons of the green peppercorns. Process until smooth, 1 to 2 minutes. Pour in cream and process again to blend. Transfer to bowl and stir in remaining teaspoon of green peppercorns. Scrape into 2-cup ramekin, cover and refrigerate at least 4 hours before serving. Let pâté stand at room temperature 30 minutes before serving.

Makes 2 cups pâté.

Cayenne-spiced pecans

2 cups pecan halves
4 tablespoons unsalted melted butter
¼ teaspoon salt
¼ teaspoon garlic powder
¼ teaspoon cayenne pepper

In 15-by-10-inch jelly-roll pan, toss pecans and butter gently to combine; drain off any excess butter. Bake in preheated, 300-degree oven 15 minutes, stirring several times. Meanwhile, in small bowl, stir together salt, garlic powder and pepper with small wire whisk to blend well. Mix into baked pecans thoroughly.

Makes 2 cups seasoned pecans.

Cilantro appetizer dip

¼ **cup fresh lemon juice**
¼ **cup water**
1 **cup fresh cilantro leaves,**
stems removed*
¼ **cup fresh shredded coconut**
¼ **cup chopped onion**
2 **tablespoons grated fresh**
ginger
2 **teaspoons canned chopped**
green chilies
1 **teaspoon sugar**
1 **teaspoon salt**
¼ **teaspoon freshly ground**
black pepper
Corn chips

If you are looking for something different in an appetizer, try this authentic Indian dip that features fresh cilantro, ginger, green chilies and lemon juice. It is zesty, brilliant green and terrific with thin fresh corn chips. A must for people who like cilantro!

In work bowl of food processor, combine lemon juice, water and ½ cup of the cilantro leaves. Puree 2 minutes. Add remaining cilantro and process until cilantro is smooth and uniform.

Add coconut, onion, ginger, green chilies, sugar, salt and pepper and process until blended, about 1 minute. Serve with fresh corn chips or pakoras (Indian onion fritters). Dip will keep up to 1 week, covered, in refrigerator.

Makes about 1 cup dip.

*Notes: When measuring cilantro leaves, press down in cup to obtain full measure.

Prosciutto-wrapped asparagus spears

1 pound fresh medium-size asparagus spears, about 24
¼ pound prosciutto, sliced paper-thin*

*C*olorful appetizers start the juices flowing even before the first bite. I like Milwaukee Chef Andy Ruggeri's brightly colored starters for that reason as well as for their delicious tastes. This vegetable-based appetizer is perfect when cooks are searching for something lighter and healthier.

Break off fibrous end of each asparagus spear, then use knife to cut spear bottom; set aside. In 10-by-12-inch skillet, heat 3 cups water to boil over high heat. Add asparagus spears, distributing evenly. Lower heat to medium and cook, uncovered, until tender and crisp, about 3 minutes. Drain off water, then quickly plunge asparagus into pan of ice water; chill until cold, about 15 minutes. Drain asparagus on paper towels.

Cut each rectangular slice of prosciutto into thirds, lengthwise, trimming fat off edges, if desired. Wrap each third around an asparagus spear, pressing firmly to hold prosciutto in place. Arrange wrapped spears on serving tray.

Makes 24 spears.

*Note: Prosciutto, air-dried Italian ham, is available at specialty markets.

Mandarin chicken and spinach bites

2 to 3 large whole skinned and
   boned chicken breasts, about
   2 pounds*
1¾ cups chicken broth
¼ cup soy sauce
1 tablespoon Worcestershire
   sauce
1 pound fresh spinach leaves
¼ cup mayonnaise
¼ cup dairy sour cream
2 teaspoons medium-hot curry
   powder
2 tablespoons chopped fruit
   chutney*
1 teaspoon freshly grated
   orange zest
2 cans (15 ounces each)
   mandarin oranges, drained

This colorful tasty offering from Chef Andy Ruggeri uses bite-sized morsels of chicken teamed with spinach and oranges and a zesty dip in a light, appealing appetizer.

In 10-inch-diameter skillet, simmer chicken breasts, broth, soy sauce and Worcestershire sauce, covered, over low heat until chicken is fork-tender, about 30 minutes. Remove chicken from broth and let cool, about 15 minutes, on platter. Cut chicken into neat, 1-inch cubes; set aside.

Rinse and stem spinach leaves; place in a colander in a deep sink. Pour 8 cups boiling water evenly over leaves, let drain about 2 minutes and allow spinach to cool.

Place 1 chicken cube at stem end of a spinach leaf (large leaves should be folded in ½ lengthwise) and wrap leaf around cube so that chicken partly shows. Secure spinach to chicken with wooden pick. Repeat with remaining chicken and spinach. Refrigerate, covered with plastic wrap, at least 1 hour. (Recipe can be prepared up to this point one day ahead.)

In small bowl, whisk together mayonnaise, sour cream, curry powder, chutney and orange zest (outer peel of orange) until completely blended. Refrigerate, covered, at least 2 hours.

To serve, stick 1 mandarin orange section on wooden pick on end of each chicken cube. Arrange chicken appetizers on round platter next to bowl of curry-mayonnaise dip.

Makes about 40 appetizers.

*Notes: Precut cubes of chicken breast, often sold as chicken tenders, can be used in place of whole breasts, but cubes should be cooked only 20 minutes.
   I prefer Major Grey's Chutney.

Focaccia

2 stems fresh tarragon
½ cup olive oil (divided)
4 tablespoons granulated
active dry yeast
2 cups warm water
(110 degrees)
4 teaspoons sugar
4 teaspoons salt
5½ to 6 cups unbleached flour
1 clove garlic, minced
1 teaspoon dried leaf oregano
¼ teaspoon red pepper flakes

*P*izza-Lovers, you'll want to try this great portable appetizer from Waukesha Chef Louie Danegelis. *Herb-infused olive oil is brushed over the homemade bread dough and the top is flavored with garlic, oregano and red pepper flakes. Make the same dough and add additional toppings like scallops, cheese and spinach and you have Crostini, another Italian appetizer favorite.*

At least 8 hours before starting rest of recipe, prepare flavored olive oil: submerge tarragon sprigs in hot water 30 seconds, drain, let cool; place tarragon in ¼ cup of the olive oil and let stand, covered, at room temperature 8 hours or overnight.

In large mixing bowl, stir yeast into warm water until it dissolves. Blend in sugar; let stand 2 minutes, until mixture begins to form small bubbles and expand. Add ¼ cup of unflavored olive oil and salt; stir to blend. Mix in flour by hand or with dough hook until you form smooth elastic dough.

Knead by hand or machine 5 minutes. Divide dough into thirds if using three 12-inch-diameter pizza pans or into halves if using 2 rectangular 15½-by-12-inch cookie sheets. *Spread bottoms of pans with enough olive oil just to moisten. Spread dough portions on pans, pat dough with olive oil and let rest, uncovered, 10 to 20 minutes in warm place. (Dough will become light and airy.)

Pat dough into round or rectangular shapes; pat with olive oil. (If dough resists stretching, snapping back to original shape, let rest 5 minutes longer. It's not necessary to stretch dough to edges of pans.) Let dough rest 20 minutes, uncovered, before baking.*

Brush dough with flavored olive oil; rub with minced garlic. Sprinkle with oregano and red pepper flakes. Bake in preheated oven at 400 degrees 10 to 15 minutes, or until dough is light brown. Remove from oven; brush again with flavored olive oil. Serve warm in wedges.

Makes 12 to 15 servings.

*Note: If you use the focaccia recipe for crostini, divide dough between four 12-inch-diameter pizza pans (or 3 rectangular cookie sheets) to get a thinner dough. Also, cut the second raising time from 20 minutes to 10.

Crostini

3 tablespoons olive oil (divided)
1 pound fresh spinach, washed, drained, stems removed
½ teaspoon Anisette, Pernod or other anise-flavored liqueur
2 cups dry white wine
18 medium-size sea scallops, cut in half horizontally
1 cooled focaccia, 12 inches diameter
½ pound Havarti cheese

Heat 1½ tablespoons of the olive oil in large skillet over medium heat. Add spinach leaves and sauté until limp and tender, about 5 minutes. Add liqueur; stir to blend flavors. Remove from skillet to plate to cool. Wipe out skillet with paper towel; add wine and remaining 1½ tablespoons oil; bring to simmer over medium heat. Add scallops and gently poach in simmering wine 2 minutes. Drain scallops.

Grill scallops on oiled grill pan (skillet with grid patterns on the bottom) or on a grill over high heat for 1 minute, just enough to flavor scallop and transfer grid marks to each surface. Set aside.

Cut round focaccia into 1½-inch squares, trimming off rounded edges. Cut Havarti into 1-inch-by-¼-inch slices. Top each focaccia square with piece of flavored spinach, grilled scallop half and cheese slice. Bake crostini on 15½-by-12-inch, ungreased baking sheet at 350 degrees about 5 minutes, or until crostini are warm and cheese begins to melt. Serve hot.

Makes 3 dozen appetizers.

Mango chutney

5 firm-ripe mangoes (about
   3 pounds)*
½ cup dark currants
½ cup fresh lime juice, strained
2 tablespoons vegetable oil
1 cup thinly sliced onion
1 large fresh, hot red chili
   pepper, seeded*
1½ cups white wine vinegar
1 cup sugar
2 teaspoons mustard seed
¼ cup minced preserved red
   ginger slices in syrup*
1 teaspoon ground cinnamon
1 tablespoon canning salt

*Q*uick appetizers are a lifesaver when you want to entertain without a lot of fuss. I have been a fan of Major Grey's Mango Chutney for years but price and availability are sometimes problems. This beautiful mango chutney comes from a gorgeous cookbook, Perfect Preserves†, that features many delectable jams, jellies and chutneys. I make this as gifts and serve it with cream cheese and crackers as an appetizer or as a flavoring in a mayonnaise-based dressing for chicken and turkey salads. It is delicious!

†*From* Perfect Preserves, © 1990 Nora Carey. Reproduced by permission of Stewart, Tabori & Chang, Publishers.

Peel mangoes; chop flesh into ½-inch pieces (makes about 4 cups); discard seeds. In large bowl, combine mangoes with currants and lime juice.

In large non-reactive (not aluminum) saucepan, heat oil over low heat until hot but not smoking. Cook onion and pepper in oil, stirring, about 10 minutes, until softened but not browned. Stir in mango mixture. Stir in vinegar, sugar, mustard seed, ginger slices, cinnamon and canning salt (has no iodine). Cook mixture over low heat, stirring, until sugar dissolves, about 2 minutes.

Bring mixture to boil, continue cooking over moderate heat 15 minutes, or until mango is soft but not pureed. Discard chili pepper. (At this point, chutney can be used immediately or frozen in straight-sided jars with 1 inch expansion space; chutney keeps frozen up to 12 months.)

Spoon chutney into 7 warm, sterilized, half-pint jars to within ¼ inch from top; wipe jar edges clean; seal jars with clean lids and rings. Fill large canning kettle (with rack) with water deep enough to cover jars at least 2 inches. Bring water to vigorous boil. Put jars of mango into kettle's rack, then add rack to boiling water, cover kettle and process 10 minutes, with water boiling vigorously. Remove and let jars cool completely before checking seals. Jars are sealed when lids are indented slightly (they make a popping noise). Carefully remove screw bands and dry off jars thoroughly for storage to avoid rust. Label with contents and date.

Makes 7 half-pints.

*Notes: Peeled nectarines can be substituted for mangoes. Wear rubber gloves when seeding peppers. Preserved red-ginger slices in syrup are available in jars at most any Asian market. Refrigerate any remaining stem ginger and syrup for use in other recipes.

Louise's brittle bread

2¾ cups all-purpose flour
2 tablespoons sugar
¾ teaspoon salt
½ teaspoon baking soda
½ cup butter or margarine, softened
8 ounces plain yogurt

Herbed cream cheese

8 ounces cream cheese, softened
½ cup unsalted butter, softened
1 clove garlic, minced or pressed
1 teaspoon dried, crumbled leaf oregano
½ teaspoon dried, crumbled leaf thyme
½ teaspoon dried, crumbled leaf basil
½ teaspoon freshly ground black pepper

Martha Giddens Nesbit shared this wonderful, crisp home-made cracker bread and accompaniment at a cooking seminar on Hilton Head Island. It is great with before-dinner wine or at a wine-tasting party. These can be made ahead and frozen for easy entertaining!

From the Savannah Collection, *by Martha Giddens Nesbit, Box 22663, Savannah, GA 31403-2663.*

In large mixing bowl sift flour, sugar, salt and baking soda together. Cut in butter until mixture has the texture of cornmeal. Mix in yogurt until dough forms a smooth ball. (All of this can be done in a food processor.) Chill 2 to 3 hours before handling or place in freezer at least 30 minutes.

Keep dough chilled, taking it out only long enough to make 1 panful of crackers. Form dough into walnut-size balls. With rolling pin, roll out each ball flat on well-floured board to a rough, 3 ½-inch square.

Bake on ungreased cookie sheet at 450 degrees 5 minutes. Skin will pucker and puff in some places. Remove to cooling rack; salt lightly. Repeat process until all dough is used. Pile "crackers" on large baking sheet. Shut off oven; when temperature has dropped to about 150 degrees, return crackers to oven and let set, with door closed, overnight. Store in plastic bags in refrigerator or freezer. Serve plain or with herbed cream cheese.

Makes about 50 crackers.

To make cream cheese put ingredients in mixer of food processor and blend (or mix on medium speed in an electric mixer). Store in covered crock in refrigerator. Chill at least 24 hours before serving so flavors can blend. Serve at room temperature.

Makes 1½ cups.

The Sunday Cook

C·O·L·L·E·C·T·I·O·N

 Soups

Mexican tortilla soup

- 2 whole chicken breasts (6 to 8 ounces each), boned and skinned
- 8 cups chicken broth (divided)
- 6 corn tortillas (6 inches in diameter)
- 1 cup corn oil
- ½ cup diced onion
- 1 teaspoon minced garlic
- 2 medium tomatoes, seeded and diced (to make about 1 cup)
- 2 tablespoons fresh lime juice, strained
- 1 avocado, peeled, pitted and diced
- ¾ cup grated Monterey Jack* cheese
  Several fresh cilantro leaves for garnish

I tasted this delicious Mexican soup with the subtle addition of fresh lime juice in an open-air restaurant in Cancun. Strips of white chicken meat, chicken broth, onion, tomatoes and garlic contribute to its marriage of good flavors. Crisp corn tortilla strips, avocado and cheese finish off this memorable taste of Mexico.

Divide chicken breasts in half lengthwise and place in microwavable dish in 2 cups of chicken broth. Cover with plastic wrap, folding back 1 corner. Microwave on high power in 600- to 700-watt microwave oven 10 to 12 minutes, rotating dish ¼ turn halfway through cooking. Remove from oven; let stand 5 minutes. Strain broth and reserve. (Chicken breast also may be grilled on lightly oiled grill over high heat, 6 minutes per side, or until juices run clear, not pink.)

When chicken is cool enough to handle, cut into ¾-inch cubes. Set aside.

Cut tortillas into ½-inch strips. In 9-inch-diameter skillet, heat oil over medium-high heat until hot. Fry tortilla strips, in batches, just until crisp. Drain on several layers of paper towels. Set aside. Discard oil from skillet. Using whatever oil still clings to skillet, sauté onion and garlic until onion is transparent, 1 to 2 minutes.

Place tomatoes, along with the sautéed onion and garlic, in heavy, 3 ½-quart kettle. Add 6 cups remaining chicken broth plus reserved chicken broth and cubed chicken. Heat until hot, about 15 minutes. Stir in fresh lime juice, ¾ of fried tortilla strips and avocado. Ladle soup into bowls; top with cheese, several cilantro leaves and sprinkle with remaining tortilla chips.

Makes 6 servings.

*Note: Fontina cheese or peppered Cheddar can be substituted for the Monterey Jack.

Photo on page 43

Black-bean turkey chili

- 1 pound ground turkey, fresh or frozen (thawed)
- 1 onion, chopped
- 1 tablespoon vegetable oil
- 1 cup chopped green bell pepper
- 2 large cloves garlic
- 1½ tablespoons chili powder
- ½ teaspoon salt
- ½ teaspoon cumin
  Dash cayenne pepper
- ¼ cup salsa
- 1 can (4 ounces) diced green chilies
- 2 cans (28 ounces each) whole tomatoes with juice, crushed
- 2 cans (16 ounces each) black beans, rinsed and drained

Readers sent me flavoring suggestions when I originally published this chili from a cookbook. They felt (and I believe they were right) that the original lacked "fire." I have adapted the original recipe to add green bell pepper, cumin, cayenne pepper and bottled salsa. I think you'll like this version.

In 6-quart pot or Dutch oven, brown crumbled turkey, onion, and green bell pepper in oil over medium-high heat, stirring to break up lumps, until turkey has lost all of its pink color and begins to brown. Drain off any excess fat.

Peel garlic and crush in garlic press; add to turkey mixture with chili powder, salt, cumin, cayenne pepper, salsa, chilies, crushed tomatoes with juice, and beans; stir well. Heat to boiling, stirring often. Reduce heat to low and simmer, stirring occasionally, 30 minutes.

Makes 6 to 8 servings.

Harvest tomato soup

3 tablespoons chopped
  shallots*
½ cup grated, peeled carrot
½ cup chopped green bell
  pepper
1 cup thin bias-cut slices
  of celery
4 tablespoons unsalted butter
1 can (49.5 ounces) chicken
  broth (divided)
4 cups fresh tomatoes, peeled,
  seeded and diced into ¼-inch
  cubes
¼ teaspoon crumbled leaf
  oregano or ¾ teaspoon fresh
  minced oregano
½ teaspoon salt
¼ teapoon freshly ground black
  pepper
1 tablespoon sugar
4 tablespoons flour
¼ loaf French or Italian bread
1 small clove garlic, halved
2 tablespoons olive oil
3 ounces crumbled feta cheese
  (optional)

A wonderfully flavored fresh tomato soup that is light and oh, so
tasty. Grated carrot, shallots,
green pepper and celery combine to
make this a rich melange of garden
goodness. Homemade croutons and
crumbled feta cheese are ideal toppers.
Don't forget this in tomato season!

In 10-inch-diameter skillet, sauté shallots,
carrot, pepper and celery in butter until vegetables are tender/crisp, 2 to 3 minutes. Stir in
4 cups of the broth, tomatoes, oregano, salt,
pepper and sugar; bring mixture to a boil.
Reduce heat to simmer; cook about 20
minutes.

In medium mixing bowl, whisk together
flour and remaining chicken broth. Slowly
whisk into tomato mixture in skillet. Cook,
stirring, until mixture thickens, 2 to 3
minutes.

Make croutons by cutting bread into ¼-inch
slices, rub surface of each bread slice with cut
side of garlic. Cut bread into ¼-inch squares.

Heat olive oil in large skillet over medium
heat. Add croutons all at once and sauté,
stirring until evenly toasted, about 5 minutes.
Drain on double layer of paper toweling.

Ladle soup into serving bowls, sprinkle with
feta cheese and top with croutons.

Makes 6 servings.

*Note: For shallots, you may substitute 3
tablespoons minced onion with 1 small clove
minced garlic.

Cheddar chowder

2 medium baking potatoes
1 large carrot, peeled
1 rib celery, rinsed and drained
1 small onion, peeled
½ teaspoon salt
¼ teaspoon ground white
  pepper
2 cups water
4 tablespoons butter or
  margarine
4 tablespoons flour
2 cups skim milk
2 cups grated sharp Cheddar
  cheese (4 ounces)
6 ounces smoked, cooked ham
  slices, diced*

A fast, flavorful food processor soup that is table-ready in 30 minutes. I like to serve this pretty soup with a crisp Waldorf salad. A true comfort fool.

Peel and quarter potatoes. In work bowl of food processor fitted with metal blade, dice potatoes using Pulse/Off button until potatoes are in ¼-inch pieces (should make about 2 cups). Remove potatoes to large kettle. Rinse work bowl, then repeat dicing process, separately, with carrots (to make ½ cup), celery (to make ½ cup) and onion (to make ¼ cup).

To potatoes in kettle, add diced carrots, celery, onion, salt, pepper and water. Cover and bring to boil over high heat; reduce heat to medium and boil about 12 minutes; set aside. *Do not drain.*

In small saucepan over medium heat, melt butter. Whisk in flour gradually, stirring until smooth. Let cook 1 minute, stirring constantly. Slowly whisk in milk; cook, stirring constantly, until thickened, about 3 minutes. Add grated cheese; stir sauce until cheese is melted.

Stir cheese sauce into *undrained* vegetables in kettle. Stir in diced ham; heat 2 minutes over medium-low heat.

Makes 6 servings.

***Note:** I used Oscar Meyer 96% fat-free ham.

Harvest bisque

1 large butternut squash,
about 2½ pounds
1 medium onion, chopped
1 tablespoon butter or
margarine
½ teaspoon curry powder
¼ teaspoon nutmeg
1 teaspoon Worcestershire
sauce
1 tablespoon smooth peanut
butter
4 cups chicken broth (divided)
½ cup heavy whipping cream or
evaporated milk
½ teaspoon salt or to taste
Dash of cayenne pepper or
to taste
8 mini pumpkins

A good squash soup in fall seems to be the right way to celebrate the abundance of the harvest season. This lovely soup from Creative Cuisine's Karen Maihofer will win over the most hesitant squash eater. A bit of peanut butter, curry and spice adds an interesting complex flavor mix.

Cut squash in half lengthwise and place, cut side down, in 13-by-9-by-2 inch baking dish. Add salted water to depth of ½ inch. Bake, uncovered, at 400 degrees until soft, 45 minutes to 1 hour, depending on size of squash; let stand until cool enough to handle. Scoop out squash into bowl, removing seeds and discarding skins; makes 4 cups cooked squash.

Meanwhile, sauté onion in butter.

In food processor, puree onion, curry powder, nutmeg, Worcestershire sauce, peanut butter, 3 cups chicken broth and all of squash until smooth; put in saucepan. (If using a blender, mix ingredients in 2 batches, adding each to saucepan when pureed.)

Whisk in remaining 1 cup chicken broth. Heat until hot, not boiling; whisk in cream and continue heating but do not boil. Season with salt and pepper.

Bake mini pumpkins in 13-by-9-by-2 inch baking pan with 1-inch water at 350 degrees for 15 minutes or until knife can pierce flesh.

Cut tops off mini pumpkins using wedge cuts, then hollow out pumpkins. Pour bisque into pumpkins. Put each pumpkin on serving plate surrounded by colorful fall leaves.

Makes 8 servings.

Italian sausage chowder

1 tablespoon olive oil
1 pound sweet Italian sausage
links
¾ cup onion, chopped
1 clove garlic, minced
2 cups beef stock or water
1 can (16 ounces) kidney
beans, drained and rinsed
1½ cups canned tomatoes with
juice, chopped, or 3 fresh
tomatoes, peeled and
chopped
1 bay leaf
¼ teaspoon dried leaf thyme,
crumbled, or ¾ teaspoon
chopped fresh thyme
¼ teaspoon dried leaf basil,
crumbled, or ¾ teaspoon
chopped fresh basil
¼ teaspoon dried leaf oregano,
crumbled, or ¾ teaspoon
chopped fresh oregano
1 white potato (not a baking
potato), peeled and diced to
make about 1 cup
½ cup chopped green bell
pepper
1 large carrot, sliced in ⅛-inch-
thick rounds (to make about
1 cup)
½ teaspoon salt or to taste
Freshly ground black pepper
1 medium zucchini, sliced in
⅛-inch-thick rounds (to make
about 1 cup)
Fresh chopped parsley for
garnish
Freshly grated Parmesan
cheese for garnish (optional)

*J*udy Marchese of Whitefish Bay shared this family favorite chowder recipe with me that she found years ago in Gourmet *magazine. You can substitute Great Northern beans for the kidney beans or finely grated cabbage for the potato, depending on your family's preferences. Serve this with a crusty Italian bread.*

Heat olive oil in heavy, 5-quart kettle over medium-high heat. Slice sausage links crosswise into ½-inch-thick slices. Brown in hot oil, turning as necessary to brown completely. Add onion and garlic; cook 2 minutes, stirring constantly. Drain off any accumulated fat.

Add beef stock, beans, tomatoes, bay leaf, thyme, basil, oregano, potato, green pepper, carrot, and salt and black pepper, stirring with wooden spoon to blend ingredients. Bring soup to boil. Cover; reduce heat to low and simmer 30 minutes. Stir in zucchini; simmer 10 minutes more, until zucchini is tender. Remove and discard bay leaf.

Just before serving, garnish with fresh parsley and Parmesan cheese, if desired.

Makes eight 1-cup servings.

Fresh fennel soup

3 fresh fennel stalks (about
2¼ pounds)*

5 tablespoons olive oil

3 medium yellow onions, sliced
to make about 1½ cups

3½ tablespoons tomato paste
(preferably imported from
Italy)

5 sprigs fresh thyme

1 small dried bay leaf

½ teaspoon dried leaf savory

9 cups good-quality chicken
stock

¼ teaspoon salt (optional)

½ teaspoon freshly ground
black pepper

3 tablespoons quick-cooking
tapioca

3 tablespoons unsalted butter

1 tablespoon fresh dill or 1
teaspoon dried dill weed

*M*ilwaukee Journal restaurant critic, Dennis Getto, shared a favorite first course soup from French author Simone Beck that he gathered in his food travels. It is exquisite hot or cold. Think of this when giving a dinner party.

Cut off upper ribs and fernlike leaves of fennel stalks (discard or use for soup). Peel outer fibrous ribs from fennel bulbs and trim off bottom of bulbs. Wash remaining bulbs (about 1½ pounds) and cut into halves, if small; into quarters, if large.

In medium saucepan, bring 4 cups water and 2 tablespoons salt to boil. Add fennel bulbs and partially cook in boiling water 5 minutes; drain off water. Rinse bulbs under cold running water; drain on paper towels. Remove center hearts of fennel bulbs, chop and reserve. Slice remaining fennel crosswise into ¼-inch-thick pieces; set aside.

In 10-inch skillet, heat olive oil, add onions and sauté over medium heat until soft and gold-flecked, about 6 minutes. Add sliced fennel; cook until vegetables begin to turn brown, about 6 minutes. Add tomato paste and simmer slowly, uncovered, stirring occasionally, about 20 minutes, or until vegetables are tender. Puree mixture in food mill or bowl of food processor or blender about 2 minutes.

Make a bouquet garni by enclosing thyme, bay leaf and savory in a 6-inch square of clean cheesecloth and securing with unwaxed dental floss.

In medium saucepan simmer fennel puree, chicken stock and bouquet garni over medium/low heat, uncovered, until soup is reduced from 3 quarts to 7 cups (will take about 1 hour and 15 minutes). Remove and discard bouquet garni. Season with salt, if desired, and pepper. Slowly stir tapioca into simmering soup. Cook until tapioca is clear, about 15 minutes. Taste, correcting seasoning if necessary. (Soup can be made to this point, then refrigerated at least 2 hours if you want to serve it cold. To complete the chilled soup, stir in 1 cup heavy whipping cream instead of butter, and add fennel hearts and dill.)

Into hot soup stir in butter, reserved chopped fennel hearts and dill. Serve hot.

Makes 6 servings.

*Note: Fennel stalks are found in the produce section of supermarkets, often near the celery.

Wild mushroom bisque

½ ounce dried morels or dried
   porcini wild mushrooms*
3 cups warm (110 degree)
   water
6 ounces fresh button
   mushrooms
6 ounces fresh brown
   mushrooms*
4 tablespoons unsalted butter
¼ cup minced shallots
¾ teaspoon salt
½ teaspoon freshly grated
   nutmeg, or to taste
2 tablespoons flour
3 tablespoons chicken stock
½ cup half-and-half
1 tablespoon fresh snipped
   chives

*G*loria Halvorsen, a Waukesha physician, is known not only for her groundbreaking medical techniques but as an accomplished cook as well. She gathers recipes from her travels and reads cookbooks voraciously. This is her version of a soup from Krabloonik, a restaurant at the base of Snowmass, Colorado. It reminded my Polish husband of the traditional wild mushroom soup served in his family on Christmas Eve.

In medium mixing bowl, soak dried mushrooms in warm water 20 minutes; drain, reserving liquid. Squeeze excess moisture from mushrooms; chop in ¼-inch pieces; set aside.

Clean and coarsely chop button and brown mushrooms. In large, heavy saucepan, melt butter over medium heat. Add shallots and cook, stirring occasionally, until soft, about 3 minutes. Add all mushrooms, salt and nutmeg.

Cook over medium heat until most of liquid evaporates, 6 to 8 minutes. Sprinkle flour over mixture and cook, stirring, 3 minutes, scraping up any bits of cooked flour from pan bottom. Whisk in chicken stock plus 2½ cups reserved wild-mushroom liquid. Bring to boil, stirring constantly. Reduce heat and boil gently until soup thickens slightly, about 20 minutes. Whisk in half-and-half; simmer 5 minutes. Sprinkle with chives and serve in soup bowls.

Makes 6 servings.

*Note: Dried wild and fresh brown mushrooms can be found at specialty food markets.

Mexican tortilla soup

Red, white & blue trifle Recipe on page 125

Recipe on page 103   **Stuffed beef tenderloin**

Recipe on page 68   **Guilt-free roasted potatoes**

46 **Banana chocolate chip pecan bread** Recipe on page 2

The Sunday Cook
C·O·L·L·E·C·T·I·O·N

■ <u>Salads</u>

Pepper-Parmesan dressing

¾ cup sour cream or
half-and-half

¼ cup light mayonnaise

½ cup freshly grated Parmesan
cheese

½ to 1 teaspoon fresh minced
garlic

1 teaspoon salt

1½ teaspoons to 1 tablespoon
fresh, coarsely ground black
pepper*

2 tablespoons buttermilk

2 tablespoons herb vinegar,
white vinegar or red wine
vinegar

2 tablespoons fresh minced
chives

2 tablespoons fresh minced
parsley

1 tablespoon finely crumbled
feta cheese

*W*ith help from two Wisconsin chefs, Terese Allen and Robert Wagner, this sought-after recipe was published in Wisconsin. It has become a favorite with my readers who love the black pepper-Parmesan taste combination.

In small bowl, combine sour cream, mayonnaise and Parmesan cheese; set aside.

With fork, mash minced garlic and salt together on small plate until it forms a paste. Add to sour cream mixture along with black pepper. Whisk in buttermilk, vinegar, chives, parsley and feta cheese, and blend. Store in covered glass jar in refrigerator. Use over mixed salad greens.

Makes about 2 cups.

*Note: Use medium grind on your pepper mill to obtain a true cracked-pepper texture and flavor.

Photo on page 118

Cucumber-dill dressing

½ cup dairy sour cream

2 teaspoons fresh lemon juice

1¼ teaspoons Dijon-style mustard

1 teaspoon finely minced fresh dill or ½ teaspoon dried dill weed

2 scallions, finely chopped

1 large cucumber, peeled, seeded and finely chopped (about 1 cup)

6 drops hot pepper sauce

¼ teaspoon salt

¼ teaspoon freshly ground black pepper

½ cup plain yogurt

Creamy dressings for seafood salads like tuna, salmon or crab are a good recipe file staple. Here's one that uses finely chopped cucumber, minced dill and plain yogurt to top your favorite fish or seafood salad. It will dress up the most mundane tuna salad.

In medium-size bowl, stir together sour cream, lemon juice, mustard, dill, scallions, cucumber, hot pepper sauce, salt and pepper. Gently fold in yogurt to blend. Refrigerate, covered, until serving time (dressing will keep up to a week in refrigerator). Use with tuna, salmon or seafood salads.

Makes 2 cups.

Photo on page 118

Sweet-fruit dressing

½ cup sugar
1 tablespoon flour
1 large egg yolk, beaten
1 cup unsweetened pineapple juice
1 tablespoon fresh lemon juice, strained
½ teaspoon grated lemon zest

An old-fashioned classic cooked dressing that begins with un-sweetened pineapple juice and lemon juice and just dresses up any fresh fruit salad beautifully. This comes from a tattered-and-torn cookbook, Favorite Recipes of Home Economics Teachers, *that I encountered while teaching in Idaho.*

In small saucepan, whisk together sugar, flour, egg yolk, pineapple and lemon juices. Stir in lemon zest. Cook over medium heat, stirring constantly, about 5 minutes, until thickened. Cool before adding to fresh or canned fruits. Store, covered, in refrigerator up to 1 week.

Makes about 1½ cups.

Photo on page 118

Raspberry vinegar

3 pints fresh or 2 bags (12 ounces each) unsweetened, loose-pack frozen raspberries
3 cups apple-cider vinegar
2 cups sugar

Make your own raspberry vinegar which is sweeter and thicker than commercial vinegars. It works beautifully in any fruit salad recipe or try it on my favorite, Rasp-berry Walnut Salad on page 51.

Place raspberries in 2-quart crock or jar. Do not use plastic. Pour vinegar over berries and let stand out overnight, covered. Strain vinegar into 1½-quart saucepan; discard berries. Stir in sugar with wire whisk. Heat in pan over medium-high heat until mixture reaches full boil. Reduce heat to simmer and simmer 10 minutes.

Pour hot vinegar into clean, sterilized jars. Lay several layers of waxed-paper squares on top of each jar. Put jar lids on top of waxed paper, then screw on metal bands to tighten.

Store in a cool place, about 65 degrees, at least 2 weeks before use; vinegar will keep up to a year.

Raspberry walnut salad

1 large head Boston lettuce
⅔ cup walnut halves
6 tablespoons safflower or
   canola oil
2 tablespoons raspberry
   vinegar*
1 tablespoon plain non-fat
   yogurt or dairy sour
   half-and-half
1 teaspoon Dijon-style
   mustard
½ pint fresh red raspberries

I absolutely love this salad, especially when raspberries are in season. Serve with grilled salmon fillets for a delightful summer repast.

At least 6 hours before serving, wash and drain lettuce leaves. Spread clean linen towel on counter; cover with layers of paper towels and lay lettuce leaves in single layer on top. Repeat paper towel and lettuce layers ending with paper towels. Roll up linen towel loosely, slip into clean plastic food storage bag. Seal bag; place in salad crisper in refrigerator 6 hours or overnight. Just before serving, tear lettuce into bite-size pieces; arrange evenly among 4 large glass salad plates. Refrigerate.

Toast walnut halves on baking sheet at 350 degrees 8 to 10 minutes. Cool walnuts on paper plate; set aside.

In small bowl, whisk together oil, raspberry vinegar, yogurt and mustard. Taste dressing and adjust seasoning if needed.*

Divide raspberries and walnut halves evenly among salad plates, then drizzle with berry vinaigrette. Serve immediately.

Makes 4 servings.

*Note: Raspberry vinegar may be purchased at specialty grocery stores or you can make your own from the recipe on page 50, which makes a heavier, sweeter vinegar than most store brands. Even commercial vinegars vary in tartness. If vinaigrette is too sharp, add 1 teaspoon sugar (or to taste) to soften flavor.

Mixed greens with glazed almonds

4 tablespoons plus 1 teaspoon sugar (divided)
½ cup sliced almonds
2 tablespoons white wine vinegar
1 tablespoon lemon juice
¼ teaspoon salt
⅓ cup vegetable oil
Dash hot pepper sauce
1 medium-size head romaine lettuce
1 medium-size head Boston or bibb lettuce
½ cup diagonally sliced celery, in ½-inch pieces
½ cup fresh bean sprouts
1 green onion, chopped fine
1 can (11 ounces) mandarin oranges, drained*
2 tablespoons chopped parsley

*C*runchy glazed almonds top this inviting mixture of salad greens, celery, fresh bean sprouts and mandarin oranges. I think this is a perfect salad to serve with some straightforward poultry entree, like a simply marinated and grilled chicken breast.

To make glaze, place 3 tablespoons plus 1 teaspoon of the sugar in small, heavy saucepan over medium heat; cook just until sugar turns honey-colored and melts, about 6 minutes, shaking pan periodically to distribute sugar evenly; do not let it brown. Remove from heat; add almonds and stir until coated. Spoon onto small, oiled cookie sheet to cool. Break apart; set aside.

Combine vinegar, lemon juice, salt, remaining tablespoon sugar, oil and hot pepper sauce in jar; cover tightly; shake well.

Separate leaves from heads of lettuce, rinse under cold water and pat dry with paper towels or spin dry with lettuce spinner and chill. Tear into bite-sized pieces. Combine in salad bowl with celery, bean sprouts, green onion and oranges. Toss with dressing; sprinkle on parsley. Before serving, sprinkle with glazed almonds.

Makes 8 to 10 servings.

*Note: Fresh orange or tangerine sections can be substituted for the mandarin oranges.

Tuscan tomato bread salad

1 pound tomatoes, washed, cored, seeded

3 cups cubed, day-old, quality French or Italian bread (in ½-inch cubes)

3 tablespoons red wine vinegar

½ teaspoon Dijon-style mustard

½ teaspoon salt

¼ teaspoon freshly ground black pepper

9 tablespoons extra-virgin olive oil

2 tablespoons finely chopped fresh basil leaves or 2 teaspoons dried leaf basil, crumbled

⅓ cup minced red onion

1 cup peeled, diced seedless cucumber

2 tablespoons capers, drained

Now don't let the sound of this salad scare you away. Home-made croutons of genuine French or Italian bread give this crisp, Mediterranean salad of in-season tomatoes and cucumbers, just the right crunch. Make this recipe anytime you are grilling meats, especially beef or lamb.

Dice tomatoes to make about 2 cups and place in large glass bowl; set aside.

Toast bread on baking sheet in preheated, 400-degree oven about 10 minutes, until golden brown. Remove from oven and cool on pan.

In small bowl, whisk together vinegar, mustard, salt and pepper. Slowly whisk in olive oil in thin stream. Add basil; mix. Pour over tomatoes. Add onion, cucumber, capers and toasted bread cubes; toss to combine. Refrigerate at least 45 minutes before serving. Toss again before serving.

Makes 6 servings.

Greek potato salad

- **2 pounds medium red potatoes, scrubbed**
- **1 teaspoon salt (divided)**
- **⅔ cup olive oil**
- **⅓ cup white wine vinegar**
- **½ teaspoon dried leaf oregano, crumbled**
- **½ teaspoon dried leaf rosemary, crumbled**
- **½ pound feta cheese, crumbled**
- **1 red bell pepper, seeded and chopped**
- **½ cup green onion, chopped**
- **½ cup Kalamata olives, pitted and chopped**
- **¼ teaspoon freshly ground black pepper**

When new potatoes are in season, toss this beautiful salad together and serve it forth with pride. It is from Susan Branch's delightfully illustrated cookbook, Vineyard Seasons.† *The combination of feta cheese, rosemary, oregano, Kalamata olives, red bell pepper and green onions is a taste sensation.*

†*From* Vineyard Seasons *by Susan Branch. Copyright © 1988 by Susan Stewart Branch. By permission of Little, Brown and Company.*

In medium saucepan, bring potatoes, 4 cups water and ½ teaspoon salt to boil over medium-high heat. Reduce heat, cover saucepan and boil gently until potatoes are tender, about 20 minutes; drain and discard water.

Place potatoes on cutting board until cool enough to handle. Coarsely cut into ½-inch pieces. Place in large salad bowl; set aside.

In large measuring cup, mix olive oil, vinegar, oregano and rosemary; pour over potatoes. Add cheese, red pepper, green onion, olives, remaining ½ teaspoon salt and black pepper. Toss gently.

Let stand at least 30 minutes at room temperature so flavors can marry. Serve at room temperature. Refrigerate leftovers, covered tightly.

Makes 8 servings.

Tuscan potato salad

3 pounds red salad potatoes
²⁄₃ cup freshly grated Parmesan cheese (about 2 ounces ungrated cheese)
1 cup ricotta cheese
4 garlic cloves, minced
½ cup red onion, very thinly sliced
½ cup olive oil
6 tablespoons cider vinegar
Salt to taste
Freshly ground pepper to taste
½ cup chopped fresh parsley

A different potato salad can be hard to find but this potato salad from the cookbook New Recipes from Moosewood Restaurant† *is worth remembering. It relies on ricotta and Parmesan cheese for flavor and a light olive oil and cider vinegar vinaigrette dressing. Because of the protein-rich cheese, remember to keep and serve this salad cold.*

†*From* New Recipes From Moosewood Restaurant. *Reprinted with permission of Ten Speed Press.*

Peel potatoes and cut in ½-inch cubes (makes about 12 cups); place in 6-quart pot; cover with water. Add 1 teaspoon salt, if desired. Bring potatoes to boil; reduce heat and simmer until just tender, about 15 minutes; drain; set aside in pot.

In medium bowl, combine Parmesan and ricotta cheeses, garlic and onion. In small bowl, whisk together olive oil, vinegar, salt and black pepper. To potatoes in pot, add cheese mixture and oil-vinegar mixture, folding over gently with rubber spatula to blend ingredients. Spoon salad into serving bowl.

This potato salad can be served warm immediately, but flavors improve on chilling. Salad will keep about 2 days in refrigerator. Keep salad cold on picnics. Sprinkle with chopped parsley for garnish before serving.

Makes 8 servings.

Syrian salad

1 large head romaine lettuce, washed, drained and chilled
1 cucumber, seedless preferred, washed
5 radishes, washed
1 red bell pepper, seeded
1 green bell pepper, seeded
1 small red onion
2 large plum tomatoes, cut in wedges
2 scallions chopped
3 ounces feta cheese, crumbled
½ cup stemmed fresh parsley, coarsely chopped
  Black olives
2 tablespoons capers (optional)
¼ cup olive oil
¼ cup freshly squeezed lemon juice
1 tablespoon wine vinegar
1 clove garlic, minced
¼ teaspoon salt
  Freshly ground black pepper to taste
  Pinch of dried mint

*W*inter salads that promise spring are almost a necessity in the midwest. This colorful, crunchy salad with Mediterranean overtones comes from the cookbook Sundays at Moosewood Restaurant†. *It is among the most popular recipes I published in the column. Do try it!*

†*Copyright © 1990 by Vegetable Kingdom, Inc. Reprinted by permission of Simon & Schuster, Inc.*

Tear chilled romaine lettuce into bite-sized pieces and place in large salad bowl. Cut cucumber and radishes into ⅛-inch slices. Slice red and green bell peppers into lengthwise strips. Slice red onion crosswise into thin rings.

Top romaine with cucumber and radish slices, bell peppers, onion rings, tomatoes and scallions; sprinkle with feta cheese, parsley, olives and capers, if desired. Toss lightly to mix.

For the dressing, combine olive oil, lemon juice, vinegar, garlic, salt, pepper and mint. Shake well in covered container to blend; drizzle over salad ingredients.

Makes 8 servings.

Nancy's miniature tomato medley

½ pound cherry tomatoes
½ pound little yellow plum
  tomatoes
1 tablespoon red wine vinegar
½ teaspoon Dijon-style
  mustard
¼ teaspoon salt
¼ teaspoon freshly ground
  black pepper
3 tablespoons canola or
  vegetable oil
1 tablespoon thinly sliced
  green onion
2 ounces blue cheese,
  crumbled

This salad was inspired by a food gift from a dear friend who sent me home with a lovely little basket piled high with yellow plum tomatoes and cherry tomatoes from her thriving garden. It is colorful, cute and oh, so delicious. And the crumbling of blue cheese is a perfect complement to beef.

Wash and then cut cherry and yellow tomatoes in half and place on large serving platter, cut sides up.

In small bowl, whisk together vinegar, mustard, salt and pepper. Slowly whisk in oil in thin stream. Drizzle salad dressing over tomatoes; sprinkle with green onion and blue cheese. Serve immediately.

Makes 6 servings.

Coleslaw with celery-seed dressing

1 medium head green cabbage,
  about 2½ pounds
¼ cup minced white onion
¾ cup finely chopped green
  bell pepper
½ cup white vinegar
½ cup sugar
½ cup low-calorie mayonnaise
1 teaspoon celery seed

Most cooks like to have a tasty and colorful coleslaw tucked away in their recipe files. This old-fashioned classic shared by Bob Rouleau is flavorful and easy to put together. The dressing is special—do try it!

Shave cabbage by slicing in very thin strips with sharp knife on cutting surface. Place in large glass serving bowl. Add onion and green pepper; set aside.

In small bowl whisk together vinegar and sugar until sugar dissolves, 2 to 3 minutes. Whip in mayonnaise until smooth and creamy. Whisk in celery seed. Pour over cabbage mixture in large bowl right before serving; toss to blend.

Makes 8 to 10 servings.

Wild rice and tortellini salad

- 1 package (6 ounces) long grain and wild rice mix*
- 1 package (9 ounces) refrigerated fresh cheese-filled tortellini*
- 3 medium tomatoes, coarsely chopped
- 2 cups broccoli florets
- ½ cup finely chopped red onion
- 1 can (6 ounces) pitted ripe olives, drained
- 1 bottle (8 ounces) Italian dressing*
- 1 tablespoon chopped fresh basil or 1 teaspoon dried leaf basil

*M*y sister-in-law, Lisa Hinde, brought this nifty salad to a family picnic. We all asked for the recipe immediately. It goes together quickly (using convenience ingredients) and travels well to family reunions or spur-of-the-moment picnics. It has been very popular with readers.

Cook rice mixture according to package directions, about 25 minutes. Chill in refrigerator about 35 minutes. Cook tortellini according to package instructions, about 5 minutes; drain off water. Chill about 45 minutes in refrigerator.

In large salad bowl, mix together tomatoes, broccoli florets, onion, olives, chilled rice, chilled tortellini and Italian dressing. Add basil, toss to blend.

Serve immediately. Refrigerate leftovers.

Makes 8 servings.

*Notes: I used Uncle Ben's Long-Grain and Wild Rice (box says Original Recipe) and DiGiorno fresh cheese-filled tortellini. I prefer Henri's Savory Italian Herb Dressing or a homemade white wine vinegar and oil dressing.

Caesar salad

2 anchovy fillets
2 medium cloves garlic, minced
1 teaspoon salt or to taste
6 tablespoons vegetable oil
2 tablespoons red wine vinegar
1 tablespoon fresh lemon juice, strained
½ teaspoon Worcestershire sauce
1 teaspoon dry mustard
1 teaspoon freshly ground black pepper
2 large heads romaine lettuce, washed, drained, torn and chilled
1 cup croutons
1 tablespoon freshly grated Parmesan cheese

Most everyone loves a good Caesar salad but concern over raw egg safety has made some cooks timid about serving this popular classic. Here's a version without the raw egg that my family has loved for years. Purists may blanch at the omission but I believe your guests will appreciate your thoughtfulness.

Drain anchovies on paper towel, then put in small bowl and mash fine with fork. Place minced garlic in wooden or glass salad bowl. Add salt. Mash into paste with back of spoon. Add mashed anchovy fillets plus vegetable oil, vinegar, lemon juice, Worcestershire sauce, dry mustard and black pepper, and mix well.

Just before serving, add lettuce. Toss well to blend with dressing. Garnish with croutons and freshly grated Parmesan cheese.

Makes 12 servings.

Citrus-pomegranate salad

2 large pink or white grapefruit,
  peeled
2 ripe avocados, peeled
1 pomegranate
6 tablespoons sugar
½ teaspoon dry mustard
¼ teaspoon salt
3 tablespoons cider vinegar
1 cup vegetable oil
2 tablespoons poppy seed
2 small heads bibb or Boston
  lettuce, washed and chilled
Watercress

Serve this salad between courses at your Thanksgiving feast and be prepared to give out copies of the recipe. It is a great way to introduce guests to bright red, crunchy pomegranate seeds. This salad looks like holiday food should look.

Cut away any white membrane from surface of grapefruit. Over a dish to catch juice, section grapefruit by cutting close to the membranes on both sides of sections. Lift out each segment in 1 piece and remove any seeds; set aside. Reserve any leftover grapefruit juice to brush on avocado slices.

Cut each avocado in half lengthwise, twisting halves in opposite directions to separate. Lift out seed; discard. Slice avocados in ¼-inch lengthwise sections; brush cut avocado with fresh grapefruit juice to prevent darkening; set aside. Cut pomegranate in half with sharp knife. Using fork, scrape seeds from white membrane, saving seeds and discarding membrane. Set seeds aside.

Make poppy-seed dressing by combining sugar, mustard, salt and vinegar in blender, food-processor bowl or medium bowl with a wire whisk. Process or beat until blended and sugar is dissolved, about 3 minutes with hand beating.

With food-processor or blender running (or whisking by hand vigorously), add oil slowly, pouring in very thin stream. Dressing will be very thick. Add poppy seed; process or whip in a few seconds.

Line 6 individual salad plates with crisp lettuce leaves and sprinkling of watercress leaves. Arrange avocado and grapefruit sections in pinwheel form on top, alternating fruits. Spoon 2 tablespoons poppy-seed dressing over each salad; sprinkle each with 1½ teaspoons pomegranate seeds.

Serve immediately.

Makes 6 servings.

Mango salad

2 heads Boston lettuce
1 bunch watercress
½ pound jicama
2 pink grapefruits
2 ripe mangoes
2 avocados
1 tablespoon chopped, fresh parsley
1 teaspoon sugar
½ teaspoon salt
½ teaspoon freshly ground black pepper
⅛ teaspoon cayenne pepper
3 tablespoons vegetable oil

Looking for something special and festive in a salad for the holiday season? Why not stretch your culinary repertoire with some somewhat exotic ingredients like jicama and mangoes in an interesting mixture of salad greens with a pink grapefruit vinaigrette? This is beautiful to serve and makes an excellent palate cleaner between the richer courses of festive foods.

Rinse and dry lettuce and watercress; remove stems from watercress; chill both greens. Tear lettuce into bite-size pieces and place in large glass salad bowl. Add watercress. Peel jicama, discarding skin. Cut into 1½-inch-long, ⅛-inch-thick julienne strips to yield about 2 cups. Add to other greens in salad bowl.

Peel grapefruits; remove and discard white pithy layer from fruit. Cut grapefruit into segments between membranes and remove fruit from membranes, then squeeze juice from fruit that clings to membranes to yield ⅓ cup; reserve. Add fruit segments to salad bowl with greens.

Peel mangoes with sharp knife. Make 1 cut all the way around fruit to pit. Then cut ¼-inch-thick wedges from mango. When all fruit has been cut from pit, discard pit. Add mango wedges to salad.

Peel avocados, cut in half, remove pits; cut avocados into ¼-inch-thick slices; add to salad bowl.

Make vinaigrette in small bowl by whisking reserved ⅓ cup grapefruit juice, parsley, sugar, salt, black pepper and cayenne until blended. Gradually whisk in vegetable oil. Drizzle vinaigrette over salad, toss gently to blend and serve immediately.

Makes 12 servings.

Cranberry-apple salad

1½ **cups fresh or frozen (unthawed) cranberries**
4 **tablespoons plus 2 teaspoons sugar (divided)**
1 **teaspoon grated orange zest**
2 **tablespoons fresh lime juice**
2 **teaspoons Dijon-style mustard**
½ **cup olive oil or vegetable oil**
2 **large Granny Smith apples, cored, coarsely chopped**
1 **cup coarsely chopped walnuts**
¼ **cup sliced green onions**
½ **cup golden raisins**
1 **head romaine lettuce or green and white kale Grated lime zest as garnish**

Karen Maihofer shared this beautiful special occasion salad in one of her popular holiday cooking lessons. It is just one of the many delicious recipes she has shared with students in her Creative Cuisine cooking classes. The lime vinaigrette is especially tasty.

Coarsely chop cranberries by hand or in bowl of food processor. In medium-size bowl, combine cranberries, 4 tablespoons of the sugar and orange zest. Cover; chill overnight.

In blender, blend lime juice, mustard and remaining 2 teaspoons sugar. Add olive oil gradually, blending until mixture is smooth.

In bowl, mix together apples, walnuts, onions and raisins; pour lime vinaigrette over all, cover and refrigerate 1 to 4 hours.

To serve, line a large platter with romaine. Spoon apple mixture onto platter leaving a 2-inch border of lettuce around edge. Make a well in center of apple salad and spoon in cranberry mixture. Garnish with grated lime zest.

Makes 8 servings.

Aunt Marie's ribbon salad

5¾ cups water (divided)
1 box (3 ounces) lime-flavored gelatin
1 can (16½ ounces) Royal Anne cherries, drained
1 box (3 ounces) lemon-flavored gelatin
15 large marshmallows
¼ cup granulated sugar
1 package (3 ounces) cream cheese, softened
1 cup heavy whipping cream, whipped
1 can (8 ounces) crushed pineapple, undrained
2 boxes (3 ounces each) cherry-flavored gelatin
2 lemons, sliced and slices cut in half, for garnish

*A*unt Marie Ressler used to bring this beautiful layered red, white and green salad to every holiday farmhouse feast. I waited for this salad every year and ate as much as my crowded dinner plate could hold. Make this salad in honor of all our aunts who made us food memories.

Bring 3½ cups of the water to a boil; set aside. Refrigerate remaining 2¼ cups of water, adding ice cubes. In small bowl, dissolve lime gelatin in 1 cup boiling water; stir to dissolve; add ¾ cup ice water; pour into bottom of oiled 11-cup ring mold. Chill until gelatin is consistency of unbeaten egg whites. Place cherries in decorative pattern in gelatin. Chill in refrigerator until firm, 30 to 35 minutes.

Meanwhile, in large bowl, dissolve lemon gelatin in 1 cup of the boiling water. While mixture is still hot, stir in marshmallows until dissolved; cool to room temperature. In separate bowl combine sugar and cream cheese, whipping with whisk until smooth; mix into lemon-gelatin mixture with whisk, blending until smooth. Fold whipped cream and pineapple into lemon-gelatin mixture. Pour all over firm (but not fully set) lime-gelatin layer; chill until firm, about 45 minutes.

Meanwhile, in another bowl, dissolve cherry gelatin in 1½ cups of the boiling water; stir in 1½ cups ice water. Pour over firm (but not fully set) lemon-gelatin layer; refrigerate until completely set, at least 2 hours. Recipe can be made a day ahead.

To serve, invert mold onto serving plate. Dip a towel in hot tap water and lay over top of mold about 1 minute; repeat until you can feel mold has loosened when you shake it gently; carefully lift off mold. Garnish with lemon.

Makes 16 to 20 servings.

Christmas crunch salad

2 cups thinly sliced cauliflower
  florets
2 cups thinly sliced broccoli
  florets
½ cup chopped pimento-
  stuffed green olives
½ cup finely chopped green or
  red bell pepper
3 tablespoons thinly sliced
  green onion
2 tablespoons fresh lemon
  juice, strained
2 tablespoons white wine
  vinegar
1 teaspoon salt
½ teaspoon sugar
⅛ teaspoon freshly ground
  black pepper
6 tablespoons vegetable oil

Traditionalists like the colors of Christmas to extend to the holiday tables. Here's a salad of non-threatening ingredients that preserves the bright red and greens of the season and, in addition, holds up well in a buffet line.

Combine cauliflower, broccoli, olives, bell pepper and onion in large salad bowl; set aside.

In small bowl, whisk lemon juice, vinegar, salt, sugar and pepper until seasonings are dissolved. Slowly whisk in vegetable oil. Pour over salad; stir to blend. Cover bowl and refrigerate 2 hours.

Makes 8 servings.

Fresh fruit salad with coconut dip

1 large ripe pineapple, washed
and drained
3 bananas, peeled
3 red or yellow Delicious
apples, washed and drained
1 tablespoon lemon juice
3 oranges, washed and peeled
1 carton (16 ounces) cottage
cheese
¼ cup plain yogurt
½ cup honey
¼ cup shredded coconut

Teaching pre-schoolers about nutrition can be a challenge but the Waukesha County Technical College's popular class, "Moms & Kids in the Kitchen," gets the lessons across. I team-taught the class with Connie Meyer and found the children receptive to different foods—as long as they helped prepare them. This salad was enormously popular with both kids and their moms.

Prepare pineapple by twisting off stalk, carefully cutting off outer peel and cutting into lengthwise quarters. Remove tough, center fibrous core with sharp knife; discard. Cut remaining pineapple into bite-size chunks. (Parents should cut pineapple for young children.)

Slice bananas into ½-inch pieces. Remove and discard apple cores and seeds but do not peel apples; cut into lengthwise quarters, then into bite-size wedges. Dip apple wedges into lemon juice in bowl to prevent apples from turning brown.

Grate zest (thin outer rind) from 1 orange to make 1 teaspoon grated zest; remove white membrane from the orange. Peel other 2 oranges; separate all oranges into sections. Remove and discard visible seeds.

Arrange fruit by type on large platter. Cover with plastic wrap; chill.

In blender container, process cottage cheese at low speed until smooth, stopping occasionally to scrape down sides of container, about 1 minute. Blend in yogurt, honey, coconut and orange rind, processing just until combined, about 10 seconds.

Place dip in serving bowl and serve with platter of prepared fresh fruit. (Or dip can be covered with plastic wrap and chilled until serving time.)

Makes 8 to 10 servings.

The Sunday Cook

C·O·L·L·E·C·T·I·O·N

■ Vegetables/
Side Dishes

Guilt-free roasted potatoes

4 large russet baking potatoes
  (about 8 ounces each)
½ cup grated Parmesan cheese
1 teaspoon dried leaf basil,
  crumbled
1 teaspoon seasoned salt
¼ teaspoon onion powder
¼ teaspoon garlic powder
  Freshly ground pepper
  Vegetable oil spray

Men who love to cook are growing in numbers—thank goodness! In our family, it is my brother-in-law, George Sunseri, of suburban Minneapolis who steals the culinary show. In this recipe of his, the fat-free potato wedges are golden brown, crunchy and filled with flavor. They are a hands-down favorite with my column readers who loved their tasty goodness, simplicity and healthfulness.

Thoroughly wash and scrub potatoes; drain on paper towels. Cut each potato into 4 lengthwise quarters. Do not rinse, so that starch on potatoes allows seasonings to stick. Set aside.

Combine Parmesan cheese, basil, seasoned salt, onion and garlic powders, and freshly ground pepper on large paper plate. Press cut surfaces of potatoes firmly into mixture; place potato slices, cut-sides-down, 2 inches apart on 15½-inch cookie sheet that has been coated with vegetable-oil spray.

Roast potatoes in preheated, 350-degree oven 30 minutes. Remove from oven, and, with metal spatula, lift and turn each potato slice so that the exposed surface is against baking sheet. Bake 30 minutes more at 350 degrees until potatoes are golden brown and crunchy. Place on warmed platter and serve immediately.

Makes 4 servings.

Photo on page 45

Oven-roasted vegetables

6 to 8 medium russet potatoes
8 large carrots, peeled
4 leeks
2 fennel stalks
5 tablespoons unsalted butter

*S*usie's Restaurant in Baraboo features this gold-tinged vegetable melange with its wonderful Brittany Baked Cod. Owner Susan Quiriconi graciously shared the recipe with me. It teams beautifully with the Savory Pot Roast (see page 105 for recipe) and is ideal in the cooler weather months.

Peel potatoes and cut into 4 lengthwise wedges. Place in large bowl with enough cold water to cover. Cut carrots into 1½-inch-long diagonal slices; place in cold water along with potatoes.

Slice ½-inch from stem end of leeks. Cut white and pale green portions in 1½-inch-long pieces; discard upper dark green portions. Rinse leeks thoroughly to remove any sand or soil; set aside.

Remove and discard fernlike foliage from fennel stalks. Trim ½-inch from stem end of fennel bulbs. Cut bulbs in half, then into ½-inch-wide wedges.

Drain water from potatoes and carrots and place in roasting pan with leeks and fennel. Preheat oven to 500 degrees. (If you have one oven, do not put in the oven at the same time the pot roast is cooking. Pull the pot roast out and let it sit on a burner on simmer while roasting the vegetables.)

Make clarified butter by melting butter in small saucepan over low heat. When completely melted, remove from heat, let stand about 5 minutes, allowing milk solids to settle to bottom. Skim foamy white butterfat from top; discard. Spoon off remaining clear yellow liquid (clarified butter) and drizzle over vegetables, stirring vegetables with wooden spoon to coat evenly. Roast at 500 degrees until golden brown, about 30 minutes.

Makes 6 to 8 servings.

Carrots-potatoes au gratin

8 small russet potatoes, peeled
6 medium carrots, peeled
1 large white onion, peeled
2 teaspoons salt (divided)
1½ cups milk
1 bay leaf
6 peppercorns
2 tablespoons unsalted butter
   or margarine
2 tablespoons flour
⅛ teaspoon ground white
   pepper
¼ teaspoon dry mustard
   (optional)
1½ cups (6 ounces) grated
   sharp Cheddar cheese
   (divided)

Miss Charlotte Rose, my home management teacher at the University of Wisconsin-Stout in Menomonie taught me to pair potatoes with their colorful root vegetable cousin, carrots. I love this dish with corned beef or baked ham.

Slice potatoes horizontally into ¼-inch-thick slices to make about 5 cups. Cut carrots on the bias into ⅛-inch-thick slices to make 2 ½ cups. Slice onion crosswise into ⅛-inch-thick slices.

In 5-quart kettle, bring 2½ cups water to boil; stir in 1 teaspoon of the salt plus sliced potatoes, carrots and all but 2 slices of the onion; cover. Cook over medium-high heat until vegetables are tender/crisp, about 6 minutes. Drain off water; set kettle of vegetables aside.

Heat milk in small saucepan just to a boil. Add remaining 2 slices of onion, bay leaf and peppercorns. Cover; let stand 5 to 10 minutes.

Meanwhile, make a roux in heavy-bottomed, medium saucepan by melting butter over medium heat. Combine flour, white pepper, dry mustard, if desired, and remaining salt with wire whisk, then whisk into melted butter, stirring constantly until mixture bubbles, about 1 minute. Let roux cool 2 minutes.

Strain milk, discarding onion rings, bay leaf and peppercorns. Gradually whisk hot milk into roux, stirring constantly, until mixture comes to a boil. Reduce heat and simmer 5 minutes. Stir in 1¼ cups of grated cheese, whisking until cheese is completely melted. Pour sauce over vegetables in kettle; fold gently to blend.

Spray 2½-quart casserole dish with vegetable-oil spray. Pour vegetable/sauce mixture into casserole; sprinkle top with remaining ¼ cup grated cheese. Cover with lid or heavy foil. Bake in preheated, 375-degree oven 20 minutes; remove cover. Bake 10 minutes more, or until top of casserole is lightly browned.

Makes 8 servings.

Wild mushrooms au gratin

½ cup fresh white bread crumbs

½ cup freshly grated Parmesan cheese

½ cup finely shredded fresh Gruyere or slightly aged Swiss cheese

3 tablespoons chopped fresh parsley

1 tablespoon chopped fresh basil

1 teaspoon chopped fresh thyme

1½ cups chanterelles, morels or brown mushrooms

2 cups fresh shiitake mushrooms

½ cup porcini or portobello mushrooms (Italian field mushrooms) or oyster mushrooms, cleaned and sliced

2 tablespoons unsalted butter

3 tablespoons sliced shallots, cut lengthwise

1 teaspoon minced garlic

⅓ cup dry sherry*

¼ cup Madeira

1¾ cups heavy whipping cream

½ teaspoon cracked black pepper

1 tablespoon kosher salt or ¾ teaspoon sea salt or iodized salt

Executive Chef, Scott Clark of Whitney's Restaurant in the Marriott Hotel at Brookfield prepared this signature dish at a March of Dimes benefit dinner several years ago. This is a side dish for special occasions.

In large mixing bowl, combine bread crumbs, cheeses, parsley, basil and thyme; set aside.

Clean and stem chanterelle and shiitake mushrooms and, if large, halve or quarter.

In 9-inch skillet over high heat on range, melt butter; when hot, add 3 types of mushrooms and sauté 5 to 7 minutes, stirring frequently but gently until golden brown. Add shallots; sauté 2 minutes more. Add garlic; sauté 1 minute. Reduce heat to medium; add sherry, Madeira, cream, pepper and salt; simmer 5 minutes.

Remove mushrooms from pan with a slotted spoon and place in mixing bowl. Over low heat, reduce sauce, stirring frequently, until sauce coats back of a wooden spoon, about 10 minutes.

Return mushrooms to sauce along with any juices that may have accumulated; stir. Divide mixture and place into 6 buttered, individual au-gratin dishes (5-by-2¾-by-⅞-inches each). Splash with a few more drops sherry and sprinkle with reserved herb-crumb mixture. Place under pre-heated broiler and broil until crust is golden brown, 30 to 60 seconds. Serve immediately.

Makes 6 single servings.

Notes: Dry Sack sherry is preferred. The herb-crumb and mushroom mixtures can be prepared 2 days in advance. Keep crumbs in an airtight container; refrigerate the mushrooms, covered. Reheat mushroom mixture in top of double boiler pan over low heat 7 to 10 minutes before the final heating in broiler.

Hanukkah potato pancakes

- 3 tablespoons unsalted butter
- 2 large baking potatoes (about 1 pound)
- 2 large eggs
- ¼ cup flour
- ¼ cup heavy whipping cream
- 2 tablespoons finely chopped onion
- ¾ teaspoon salt
- ¼ teaspoon freshly ground black pepper
- 2 tablespoons extra virgin olive oil or vegetable oil
- 2 medium red or Golden Delicious apples
- ½ pound feta or goat cheese*

*T*raditional foods, such as potato pancakes, have become staples of Hanukkah, the Jewish festival of lights. These potato pancakes prepared at Ecole de Cuisine in Mequon in an appetizer class are the prettiest, tastiest potato pancakes you will ever eat. With the help of several Milwaukee kosher cooks, the recipe has been adapted for Hanukkah. (Coarsely grating the potatoes—I use a French Mouli-Julienne hand grater with medium blade—is the secret to their incredible taste and texture.)

Start by clarifying butter for use later in frying apples. (Clarified butter can be heated to a higher temperature without burning.) Melt butter in small saucepan over low heat until completely melted; remove from heat and let stand about 5 minutes, allowing milk solids to settle to bottom. Skim foamy white butterfat from top; discard. Spoon off clear yellow liquid (clarified butter), about 2 tablespoons, and set aside.

Peel and shred potatoes with grater or with medium shredding blade of food processor. (A French Mouli-Julienne hand grater with medium blade works well.) Press potatoes between layers of thick absorbent towel to absorb extra moisture.

In large mixing bowl beat eggs, flour, whipping cream and onion with electric mixer on medium speed (or whisk by hand); stir in shredded potato, salt and pepper.

In large 10-inch or 12-inch-diameter skillet over medium heat, heat oil until hot. Add potato mixture, 2 tablespoons at a time, forming ovals about 1½ inches apart. Sauté pancakes on medium heat on both sides until they are cooked through, 7 to 8 minutes total. Repeat with remaining batter; keep cooked pancakes warm by spreading out on paper towels on top of cookie sheet and placing in 200-degree oven.

Core and slice each apple into 8 lengthwise slices; do not peel. In medium skillet over medium heat, sauté apples in 2 tablespoons reserved clarified butter until golden brown, about 10 minutes.

To serve, top each pancake with 1 apple slice, then with pieces of crumbled cheese (or slices of goat cheese). Pancakes are best served immediately, but they can be made up to 3 hours in advance, then reheated at 400 degrees 4 minutes.

Makes 16 appetizer-size pancakes.

*Note: Kosher feta cheese is sold at Kosher markets.

Oven-fried zucchini spears

- 2 medium-size zucchini or yellow summer squash (7 to 8 ounces each)
- 3 tablespoons dried bread crumbs
- 1 tablespoon grated Parmesan cheese
- 1 teaspoon dried leaf oregano, crumbled
- ½ teaspoon dried basil, crumbled
- ¼ teaspoon garlic powder
- 1 teaspoon dried summer savory, crumbled
- ⅛ teaspoon freshly ground black pepper
- 2 teaspoons corn oil
- 2 tablespoons water
  Prepared marinara sauce (optional)

I've never published a cookbook without at least one zucchini recipe in it. This great summertime vegetable dish uses a healthy amount of zucchini baked in flavorful crumbs and served, ideally with a marinara sauce.

From The Sage Cottage Herb Garden Cookbook. *Copyright © 1991 by Dorry Baird Norris. Published with permission of Globe Pequot Press.*

Wash and pat dry zucchini. Do not peel. Cut into eighths lengthwise, then into halves crosswise to get finger-size lengths of squash; set aside.

On wax paper, mix together crumbs, cheese, oregano, basil, garlic powder, summer savory and pepper; set aside.

In small bowl, mix oil and water, then toss zucchini spears in mixture to moisten surfaces. Roll spears in crumb mixture, covering all sides, then arrange on 13-by-12-inch cookie sheet that has been sprayed lightly with vegetable oil spray.

Bake in preheated, 475-degree oven 7 minutes, or until spears are lightly browned. Turn spears over; bake 3 minutes more. Serve immediately with hot prepared marinara sauce (a tomato and herb-based sauce), if desired.

Makes 4 servings.

Spaghetti squash with tomato sauce

- 4 medium tomatoes (about 1¼ pounds)
- ½ teaspoon leaf basil, crumbled, or 1½ teaspoons minced fresh basil
- ½ cup chopped green onions
- 2 cloves garlic, minced (about 1 teaspoon)
- ¾ teaspoon salt
- ⅛ teaspoon freshly ground black pepper
- 1 tablespoon olive oil
- 1 spaghetti squash (3½ pounds)
- Grated Parmesan or Romano cheese (optional)

Dan and Karen Scheel, owners of The Elegant Farmer market in Mukwonago eat what they grow on their pick-your-own plots in the Waukesha County countryside. In fall, that means they prepare all kinds of squash in a variety of tasty ways. Try Karen's recipe for spaghetti squash with an uncooked tomato-and-basil sauce. It is light and lovely!

Wash, drain and core tomatoes, then chop into ½-inch pieces; combine in medium mixing bowl with basil, onions, garlic, salt and pepper. Drizzle olive oil over mixture, then gently stir (makes about 3 cups sauce). Refrigerate, covered, 30 to 60 minutes, stirring every 15 minutes to blend flavors.

Meanwhile, cut squash in half lengthwise with sharp, heavy knife; scoop out seeds and discard. Place squash halves, cut-side-down, in 13-by-9-by-2 inch glass baking dish. Add water to come up to a depth of ½ inch (about 3 cups). Bake in preheated, 350-degree oven until squash feels soft to the touch, about 45 minutes. Remove from oven and carefully turn squash cut-sides up. Use a fork to remove spaghetti squash strands from shells to a warm serving platter. Discard squash shells.

Serve chilled tomato sauce over squash. Sprinkle with Parmesan cheese, if desired.

Makes 4 servings.

Steamed artichokes with mustard-dill sauce

4 large artichokes (12 ounces each)

2 tablespoons Dijon-style mustard

½ cup tarragon vinegar

½ teaspoon freshly ground black pepper

½ teaspoon sugar

1 cup extra-virgin olive oil

1 tablespoon fresh dill, minced

One of my family's favorite first courses, these easily prepared steamed artichokes with a pleasantly piquant vinaigrette make for a leisurely paced dinner. We often eat these standing at the kitchen island while we prepare the main course or set the table. An ideal way to introduce artichokes to children or adults.

In 4-quart stainless steel or enamel kettle, place artichokes, stem side down (fitted snugly so they don't pop up in cooking). Add cold water to cover artichokes plus 1 teaspoon salt and 1 thin slice fresh lemon (seeds removed), if desired. Bring water to boil over high heat; reduce heat to medium and boil gently about 40 minutes, or until artichoke is tender. (To test for doneness, leaves of artichoke should pull off easily.) Remove artichokes with tongs; turn upside down in colander to drain.

In small bowl, whisk together mustard, vinegar, pepper and sugar until blended. Slowly whisk in olive oil, adding in a thin stream until mixture thickens. Whisk in dill. Serve immediately with either hot or cold artichokes.

Makes 4 servings.

Cucumbers in cream sauce

4 cucumbers (each 5 inches long)
1 medium red or white sweet onion, peeled
1 tablespoon salt
6 tablespoons mayonnaise
5 tablespoons buttermilk
3 tablespoons white vinegar
½ teaspoon sugar (optional)
1 tablespoon snipped fresh dill weed
½ teaspoon freshly ground black pepper (optional)

My mother, Inez Hinde, has been making this lovely cucumber salad for as many years as I can remember. She builds her mayonnaise-based sauce out of whatever ingredients she has on hand, adding sour cream, buttermilk, or milk, as supplies dictate. She frequently slices fresh garden tomato wedges into the dish right before serving. Our family loves it!

Wash and lightly peel cucumbers (leaving some peel intact for color). Slice into ⅛-inch-thick crosswise slices (makes about 4 cups); set aside. Cut onion in lengthwise slices about ⅛ inch thick (to make about 1 cup).

In large glass mixing bowl, stir salt into 5 cups ice water until salt dissolves. Stir in cucumber and onion slices. Let stand at least 30 minutes at room temperature, then drain, discarding saltwater. Place cucumbers and onions in pretty glass bowl; set aside.

In small bowl, combine mayonnaise, buttermilk, vinegar, sugar, fresh dill and pepper, if desired. Whisk to blend until mixture is smooth. Pour over cucumbers and onions; stir to blend. Chill in refrigerator, covered, until serving time (no longer than 24 hours).

Makes 8 servings.

Southwest bean bake

4 slices extra-lean bacon
1 cup diced onion
1 teaspoon minced fresh garlic
1 jar (2 ounces) chopped
  pimentos, undrained
⅛ teaspoon dried leaf oregano
1 can (15 ounces) black beans,
  drained and rinsed
1 can (15 ounces) Great
  Northern beans, pink or pinto
  beans, drained and rinsed
½ cup mild picante sauce or
  chunky salsa
1 cup chicken broth
½ teaspoon salt or to taste
⅛ teaspoon freshly ground
  black pepper

Baked bean dishes are a picnic and potluck staple. But sometimes, cooks want to give this popular side dish a different slant. This mixed bean dish uses black beans with other bean varieties and salsa for some spunk. It is lower in calories than its baked bean counterparts.

In 9-inch skillet, fry bacon strips over medium heat until crisp, about 5 minutes. Remove bacon to paper towel; drain, cool, then crumble.

Pour off all but 1 teaspoon bacon fat from skillet. Add onion and garlic, stirring and cooking over medium heat until onion is translucent, about 3 minutes. Remove skillet from heat; add pimentos, oregano, two types of beans, picante sauce, chicken broth, salt and pepper.

Place mixture in 1½-quart casserole dish; sprinkle crumbled bacon over top. Bake at 350 degrees 25 minutes, or until dish is heated through.

Makes 6 to 8 servings.

The Sunday Cook
C·O·L·L·E·C·T·I·O·N

Chicken with 40 cloves of garlic

1 chicken (3½ to 4 pounds),
   rinsed, cut in pieces, skinned
1 tablespoon unsalted butter
¼ cup plus 1 tablespoon olive
   oil (divided)
1 teaspoon salt
Freshly ground black pepper
40 cloves garlic, unpeeled,
   separated (about 3 bulbs)
½ cup dry white wine
1 teaspoon dried thyme leaves,
   crumbled
½ teaspoon dried leaf sage,
   crumbled
½ teaspoon dried leaf rosemary,
   crumbled
1 tablespoon fresh parsley,
   minced
4 small bay leaves
½ loaf French bread

My reputation as the Sunday Cook *really began with the publishing of this somewhat startling recipe. It generated more pros and cons in the dialogue column of* Wisconsin *magazine than anything else I printed. Most of the readers readily converted into garlic lovers after tasting the buttery cloves that are slowly baked in an herb-and-olive oil wine sauce. Try it—you'll like it.*

Pat chicken pieces dry with paper towel. Heat butter and 1 tablespoon of the olive oil in large, cast-iron Dutch oven or oven-proof skillet. Brown chicken in batches (don't crowd) over medium-high heat about 5 minutes on all sides. Season with salt and pepper. Remove to plate lined with paper towels.

Pour off all accumulated fat from Dutch oven. Scatter garlic cloves over bottom of Dutch oven. Place chicken over garlic.

Pour wine and remaining ¼ cup olive oil over chicken; sprinkle with thyme, sage, rosemary, parsley and bay leaves. Cover pan tightly with heavy aluminum foil; and then lid.

Bake at 375 degrees 30 minutes. Carefully remove lid and foil; baste with oil-wine mixture. Replace foil and lid; bake 30 minutes more.

Meanwhile, slice bread into ¼-inch-thick slices. Toast on baking sheet in oven at 375 degrees 10 to 15 minutes, until crisp.

Before serving, remove and discard bay leaves. Spoon chicken, sauce and several whole cloves of garlic onto each serving plate. Squeeze garlic directly out of skins onto toasted bread, discarding skins and eating garlic paste as you would a pâté.

Makes 4 to 5 servings.

Featured on the cover and page 117

Grilled chicken breast salad

- **2 tablespoons Dijon-style mustard**
- **1½ teaspoons fresh minced parsley**
- **¼ cup balsamic vinegar**
- **1½ teaspoons cracked black pepper**
- **¾ teaspoon honey**
- **¼ teaspoon minced garlic**
- **¼ teaspoon fresh minced rosemary (optional)**
- **½ cup olive oil**
- **¼ cup walnut oil or hazelnut oil***
- **¼ cup chopped walnuts Kosher or iodized salt to taste**
- **2 whole chicken breasts (8 ounces each), skinned, boned and halved lengthwise**
- **1 to 2 tablespoons vegetable oil**
- **8 cups chilled mixed greens torn in bite-size pieces* Garnishes***

Innovative, cutting edge dishes are the signature of Cafe Knickerbocker chef, Robert Wagner. This popular luncheon salad of warm, grilled chunks of chicken surrounded by picturesque ingredients is a definite crowd-pleaser. I've eaten this many times and still would order it at the Cafe. It is that good!

In medium bowl, mix mustard, parsley, vinegar, black pepper, honey, garlic and rosemary with wire whisk. Slowly whisk in olive oil and walnut oil, whisking constantly to create an emulsion of oil and vinegar. Add walnuts and salt; set aside.

Lightly brush chicken halves with vegetable oil. Grill on an outdoor grill over high heat or broil in oven at 500 degrees about 5 minutes per side, turning once. Chicken is done when its liquid runs clear, not pink, when breasts are pierced. Let stand 5 minutes. Cut in 1-inch bias chunks.

Divide greens evenly among 4 chilled salad plates. Place one-fourth of chicken chunks on top of each plate. Drizzle with vinaigrette. Garnish according to personal tastes.

Makes 4 servings.

Notes: Flavored oils can be purchased at specialty stores. You can use Boston lettuce, endive, romaine, green and red leaf lettuce for greens. Garnishes can include sliced onions, red pepper, walnut halves, alfalfa sprouts, baby corn, cherry tomatoes and edible flowers.

Stuffed chicken breasts

12 whole boned chicken breasts
(6 ounces each)
8 teaspoons salt (divided) or to
taste
Fresh ground black pepper to
taste
2 packages (10 ounces each)
frozen chopped spinach,
thawed, drained
3 cups shredded Swiss cheese
(12 ounces)
1½ cups ricotta cheese
1 large onion, finely chopped
6 hard-cooked eggs, chopped
2 large cloves garlic, crushed
2 heaping tablespoons green
peppercorns, drained
3 sticks (1½ cups) plus 12
tablespoons unsalted butter
2 packages (16 ounces each)
frozen phyllo dough leaves,
thawed at room temperature*
Madeira sauce

Madeira sauce

6 tablespoons unsalted butter
6 tablespoons flour
6 tablespoons dry Madeira
wine
3 cups chicken broth
1 cup dairy sour cream
2 tablespoons tomato paste
1 cup chopped chives or green
onion tops
1 teaspoon salt or to taste
White pepper to taste

*R*emember this beautiful make-ahead main dish the next time you want to entertain a crowd. Golden brown phyllo dough-wrapped chicken breasts sport a tasty filling of spinach, cheeses, herbs and green peppercorns. Make them in advance; freeze them in individual portions and you are ready to entertain with a minimum of fuss. A favorite recipe from Waukesha cook, Sue Fox, who is known for her skills as a gracious hostess and exceptional cook.

Skin chicken breasts and split lengthwise so you end up with 24 chicken-breast halves; with meat mallet, pound each half to about ⅛ inch thick, into about a 3½-by-5 inch rectangle. Using about ¼ teaspoon salt per breast and pepper to taste, sprinkle over all chicken breasts (this is optional, depending on your seasoning preferences); set aside.

In large bowl mix spinach, Swiss and ricotta cheeses, onion, eggs, garlic, peppercorns and remaining 2 teaspoons salt until well-mixed and peppercorns are well-distributed. (At this point, this bowl of stuffing and the chicken breasts placed on a baking sheet may be covered and refrigerated overnight.) You should have 8 cups stuffing. Spread ⅓ cup stuffing over each breast. Starting at one end, roll up each breast jelly roll-style, folding in sides as you roll, if possible.

In small saucepan over medium heat, melt 3 sticks butter. Place 1 rectangular sheet of phyllo dough on damp towel (keep remaining phyllo covered with another damp cloth) and brush lightly with melted butter. Fold in half crosswise, with buttered side in. Turn phyllo so narrow end faces you. Place 1 chicken roll about 2 inches from narrow end of dough; top chicken with 1½ teaspoons cold butter; roll phyllo dough around chicken once, then fold in sides of dough and continue rolling until all of phyllo sheet is wrapped around chicken.

Repeat with rest of chicken rolls and 23 phyllo leaves. (You will have phyllo leaves left over for other uses.)

Place the 24 chicken rolls about 1 inch apart on 2 ungreased, 16-by-11-by-1-inch baking sheets (or jelly roll pans), seam sides down. Brush tops lightly with remaining melted butter. Place in center of oven and bake at 400 degrees 25 to 30 minutes, or until golden.

(Or, you can freeze half or all of chicken rolls, uncovered, in single layer on baking sheet until firm, 1 to 2 hours; then wrap each chicken roll securely in heavy aluminum foil. Store in freezer. To bake, first defrost on baking sheets to room temperature, then remove foil.)

To make Madeira sauce melt butter in medium saucepan. Add flour and cook, stirring until mixture is golden, about 3 minutes. Remove from heat; whisk in Madeira and broth. Return to heat and cook, stirring until mixture boils and thickens, about 5 minutes.

In small bowl, mix sour cream and tomato paste; stir in ¼ cup of hot Madeira-butter mixture, then pour all into saucepan. Stir in chives, salt and white pepper. Remove from heat.

If not serving immediately, place wax paper on top to keep skin from forming. Sauce may be kept warm by putting saucepan in larger pan of hot water. If you still need to reheat sauce, remove original saucepan from water, place over low heat and slowly bring to desired temperature. Do not boil.

To thin, add more Madeira or broth.

Drizzle Madeira sauce over cooked chicken breasts; serve immediately; pass remaining sauce.

Makes 24 one-roll servings.

Note: I used Athens Food brand phyllo dough leaves.

Chicken enchiladas

- 2 whole chicken breasts, 6 to 8 ounces each, split in half along bone
- 2 ribs celery, cut in 1-inch pieces
- 1 cup plus 6 tablespoons chopped white onion (divided)
- 3 large cloves peeled garlic (divided)
- 2 cups water
- 2 teaspoons salt (divided)
- 1¼ teaspoons freshly ground black pepper (divided)
- 2 teaspoons ground cumin (divided)
- 1 tablespoon chopped cilantro (optional)
- 8 packaged tortillas (corn, flour or blue-corn), each 6 inches in diameter
- 2½ tablespoons corn oil
- 3 tablespoons flour
- 2 cups chicken stock or broth
- 2 cans (4 ounces each) diced green chilies
- 4 cups shredded Cheddar or Monterey Jack cheese
- 1 cup chopped green onions

*C*ookbooks often stem from good causes and one of my favorites does exactly that. Orange Tree Imports Cookbook† *was put together by the talented staff of the Orange Tree Imports Cooking School in Madison to benefit the Ronald McDonald House in the city. The cookbook reflects the ethnic diversity of this great university city and the recipes are delightfully different from the ordinary. This recipe shared by Tim Guilfoil who runs Pasqual's Southwestern Style Deli in Madison is a great favorite.*

†*From* Orange Tree Imports Cookbook, *1721 Monroe Street, Madison, WI 53711.*

Place chicken-breast halves in 8-by-10-inch microwaveable dish; add celery, 4 tablespoons of the chopped onion, 2 cloves garlic and water. Cover with plastic wrap, folding back one corner. Microwave on high power in 600- to 700-watt microwave oven* 10 to 12 minutes, rotating dish ¼ turn halfway through cooking (chicken is done when juices run clear, not pink). Remove from oven; let stand 5 minutes.

Put chicken on plastic cutting surface to cool; remove skin and discard; then cut chicken away from bones. Shred chicken with fork and put in mixing bowl; add 1 teaspoon of the salt, ¼ teaspoon of the pepper and 1 teaspoon of the cumin. Mix in cilantro, if desired, and 2 tablespoons of the onion.

Heat tortillas in microwave according to package instructions until soft and pliable. Lay tortillas out on flat surface. Divide chicken mixture evenly among 8 tortillas; roll as tight as possible; place in 13-by-9-by-2-inch pan; set aside.

Heat corn oil in medium saucepan over medium-high heat until oil is hot, about

1 minute. Mince remaining garlic clove and add to oil; stir in 1 cup chopped white onion; sauté until tender, about 2 minutes. Reduce heat to low; add flour and stir constantly 3 to 4 minutes. Do not let mixture brown.

In glass measuring cup, heat chicken stock in microwave until almost boiling, about 5 minutes. Add to onion-flour mixture in saucepan slowly, stirring constantly. Cook over medium-high heat until mixture thickens, 1 to 2 minutes. Stir in green chilies, remaining 1 teaspoon salt, 1 teaspoon freshly ground black pepper and 1 teaspoon cumin.

Cover each enchilada with about ½ cup of chili sauce; sprinkle with cheese and green onions. Bake at 350 degrees in preheated oven 20 minutes. Serve immediately.

Makes 4 servings.

*Note: If microwave ovens with lower wattage are used, cooking times need to be increased.

Chili-brushed turkey breast

2 tablespoons orange juice

1 tablespoon grated orange zest

1 tablespoon chili puree with garlic*

1 tablespoon vinegar

1 tablespoon minced fresh cilantro*

½ teaspoon ground cinnamon

½ teaspoon salt

¼ teaspoon freshly ground pepper

1 fresh or frozen turkey breast (5 to 6 pounds), thawed*

3 tablespoons unsalted butter, melted

Turkey isn't just for Thanksgiving anymore, it is a year-round favorite source of protein. When I don't want to fuss with a whole bird I like to roast a fresh turkey breast with this flavorful chili-based rub that adds pizazz to an otherwise mild main dish. This roasts up to a gorgeous golden brown with memorable multiple flavors.

In small bowl, whisk orange juice, orange zest, chili puree, vinegar, cilantro, cinnamon, salt and pepper to blend; set aside.

Rinse turkey breast inside and out; dry with paper towels. Place turkey in small roasting pan, skin side up. Brush melted butter all over turkey skin. Pour reserved chili sauce over turkey, brushing lightly to distribute evenly and cover surface.

Roast turkey at 350 degrees, allowing 15 to 18 minutes per pound (1½ hours for a 6-pound breast). If turkey begins to over-brown, make a tent of aluminum foil and loosely cover turkey. If using an instant-read thermometer, insert thermometer in thickest part of breast. Thermometer should register 170 to 175 degrees when turkey is done.

Let turkey breast stand 20 minutes before carving.

Makes 12 servings.

*Notes: Refrigerate chili puree after opening and use in Oriental recipes. You can substitute fresh parsley for cilantro. Frozen turkey breast should be thawed overnight in refrigerator.

Asian duck breast

- 6 whole boneless duck breasts, about 12 ounces each, cut in halves
- 1 tablespoon Oriental brown bean paste (sauce) or plum sauce*
- 1 clove garlic, smashed or minced
- 3 tablespoons soy sauce
- 1 tablespoon Hoisin sauce
- 2 tablespoons dry sherry or white wine
- 1 tablespoon sugar
- ½ teaspoon Five Spice powder
- 2 tablespoons chicken stock
- 1 tablespoon vegetable oil

Plum chutney

- Zest from 1 orange
- ¾ cup granulated sugar
- ½ cup brown sugar
- ½ teaspoon ground ginger
- ½ teaspoon ground cinnamon
- ½ teaspoon salt
- 1 cup apple-cider vinegar
- 1½ medium red onions, coarsely chopped
- 1 Granny Smith apple, coarsely chopped
- 4 large fresh plums or canned, drained Italian prune plums
- ¼ cup dried currants

*C*hef Louie Danegelis of Waukesha is a joy to watch work with food. He is meticulous with details and his artful creations reflect that care. Try his pretty Oriental-style duck breast and fresh plum chutney accompaniment. Frozen duck breasts are available at specialty food stores like V. Richards in Brookfield, Wisconsin.

Trim off excess duck skin; place breasts in 13-by-9-by-2-inch glass baking dish. In bowl, mix brown bean paste, garlic, soy sauce, Hoisin sauce, sherry, sugar, Five Spice powder and chicken stock. Pour over duck breasts, coating well. Cover and marinate in refrigerator overnight. Let stand at room temperature for 30 minutes before cooking.

Heat oil in large skillet until hot. Drain breasts, discarding excess marinade. Sear breasts, skin-side-down, over medium-low heat until skin has browned, 5 to 8 minutes. Drain off fat; discard. Turn breasts and cook 3 to 5 minutes more.

Remove skillet from heat, cover and let set 5 to 8 minutes, allowing duck breasts to "finish" to medium doneness. Baste breasts with any cooking liquid remaining in pan. Serve with plum chutney.

Makes 6 servings.

*Notes: Brown bean paste (sauce) is available in Oriental sections of large supermarkets.

To make chutney cut zest into slivers. In 4-quart saucepan over low heat, combine zest, sugars, ginger, cinnamon, salt and vinegar, stirring constantly until mixture boils, about 5 minutes. Mix in remaining ingredients, cook over medium-high heat until mixture boils. Reduce heat and simmer 50 to 60 minutes, stirring occasionally, until fruit is soft. Refrigerate in glass jars.

Makes 4 cups.

Shrimp & sausage boil

- 2 cups prepared chili sauce
- ¾ cup fresh lemon juice
- 3 tablespoons horseradish
- 1 teaspoon grated onion
- 1 tablespoon Worcestershire sauce
- 6 drops of hot pepper sauce
- 3 pounds medium-size raw shrimp, unshelled
- 1 cup unsalted butter (divided)
- 3 pounds smoked sausage, cut into 1-inch chunks
- 10 new potatoes (1-1½-inches in diameter), unpeeled, scrubbed
- 10 small sweet onions, about 1-inch diameter
- 10 ears fresh sweet corn, broken into thirds

Low country residents of the coastal plains of North and South Carolina and Georgia have been fixing this casual feast for years and have called it Frogmore Stew or Low Country Shrimp Boil. Whatever you call it, I am grateful to Savannah cookbook writer Martha Giddens Nesbit who introduced me to this glorious summer food. You can make this for a crowd using an enamel canner on top of a backyard grill. Follow the directions and times exactly for a perfect laid-back feast.

Make sauce for shrimp by mixing chili sauce, lemon juice, horseradish, grated onion, Worcestershire and hot pepper sauce in medium bowl with wire whisk. Chill until serving time.

Rinse shrimp at least 3 times.

In 12-quart pot, bring 7 quarts of water and ½ cup of the butter to boil over high heat. Add sausage chunks, reduce heat to medium and boil gently about 15 minutes. Meanwhile, with vegetable peeler, remove one strip of potato peel from center of each potato; add potatoes to pot with sausage and boil 8 minutes more. Then add onions and corn and boil 6 minutes more, or until almost tender. Add shrimp and boil until shells turn pink and shrimp is opaque white, 3 to 4 minutes. Drain off cooking liquid and discard unless you want to cook more corn or ingredients for second helpings.

Melt remaining ½ cup of butter in small pot; serve with corn.

Spread cooked sausage, potatoes, onions, corn and shrimp on large platter and let people help themselves. Serve prepared horseradish-cocktail sauce with shrimp.

Makes 10 servings.

Photo on back cover

Shrimp pilaf

1¼ cups uncooked Basmati
    rice (Texmati)
2 cups cold water
2 teaspoons salt (divided)
2 to 3 tablespoons vegetable
    oil
1 tablespoon unsalted raw
    cashews
1 tablespoon unsalted raw
    almonds
3 medium yellow onions,
    chopped to make about
    1½ cups
2 to 3 bay leaves
½ teaspoon ground red chili
    pepper, or to taste
¼ teaspoon tumeric
1 teaspoon ground coriander
1 teaspoon garam masala
½ cup tomato sauce or 2 fresh
    tomatoes, peeled and diced
1 tablespoon garlic, minced
1 tablespoon grated fresh
    ginger
1 pound raw, medium shrimp
    (31 to 35), peeled and
    deveined

Authentic Indian food, wonderfully fragrant with Indian herbs and spices is shared by Greenfield residents, Anjali and Sameer Vijaykar from the southern state of Andhra Pradesh. Indian rice, spices and other edibles are found in Milwaukee at the Indian Groceries & Spices-International Bazaar at 4733 W. North Avenue. A beautiful main dish for the adventurous palate.

In medium-size, heavy saucepan, combine rice, water and 1 teaspoon of the salt. Bring to boil over medium-high heat; reduce heat to simmer and cook, covered, 15 to 20 minutes. Cool to room temperature; refrigerate, covered, until time to use.

In wok or heavy, 10-inch-diameter sauté pan, heat oil until hot over medium-high heat; add cashews and almonds; sauté until browned, about 30 seconds. Remove from oil with slotted spoon to paper towel; set aside.

Add onion and bay leaves to oil in pan and sauté gently until onion is golden, about 3 minutes. Add chili pepper, tumeric, coriander, garam masala and remaining 1 teaspoon salt; stir 1 minute. Add tomato sauce, stirring to blend. (If using fresh tomato, cook 2 minutes to eliminate raw flavor of tomato.)

With fork, mash garlic and ginger together in cup to form paste; add with shrimp to onion mixture and cook, over medium heat, stirring constantly, until shrimp are opaque and thoroughly cooked, about 3 minutes.

Add reserved rice to mixture; stir-fry to blend and heat thoroughly, about 3 minutes. Remove bay leaves. Add reserved nuts.

Makes 4 to 6 servings.

Shrimp and scallop kebabs

1 **pound fresh large shrimp (about 16 to 20 per pound)**
1 **pound large sea scallops (size of quarter to fifty-cent piece)**
8 **ounces whole fresh mushrooms, washed, dried and stems trimmed**
½ **cup extra virgin olive oil or vegetable oil**
¼ **cup fresh lemon juice**
2 **garlic cloves, minced**
2 **teaspoons dried leaf oregano, crumbled**
Fresh oregano for garnish
Lemon wedges for garnish

A family favorite for summer birthdays and overnight guests, this pretty pink-and-white seafood entree pleases nearly everyone. Marinate the seafood and mushrooms in a mixture of oil, fresh lemon juice, garlic and oregano, grill quickly and serve with your favorite pasta and crisp green salad. A lemon ice would be a lovely dessert.

Peel shrimp, leaving tails attached. Devein (remove dark vein on back of shrimp) by using your fingers and paper towel to draw out vein. Place shrimp, sea scallops and whole mushrooms in large, resealable plastic bag.

In small bowl, combine oil, lemon juice, garlic and oregano; whisk to combine. Pour over seafood and mushrooms in bag; seal bag tightly and shake gently. Place bag on a tray in refrigerator and marinate 4 to 6 hours or overnight, occasionally redistributing ingredients inside. Drain well, reserving marinade.

On each skewer, alternate shrimp, mushroom and scallops, ending with a shrimp; leave about an inch of room on each end.

Place skewers on lightly oiled hot grill about 6 inches from coals or heating element. Grill, basting with reserved marinade and turning once, until shrimp and scallops are opaque throughout, 5 to 10 minutes. Watch carefully!

Kebabs may be broiled by placing under red-hot broiler element, either 4 inches from element at top of oven or at lowest possible broiling level if broiler element is at bottom of your oven; broil 2 to 4 minutes per side, turning once.

Garnish with fresh oregano and lemon wedges.

Makes about 4 servings.

Scallops Provencale

3 tablespoons unsalted butter (divided)

1 tablespoon finely chopped onion

2 large ripe tomatoes, peeled, seeded and diced (1 cup)

⅛ teaspoon dried leaf thyme, crumbled

4 to 5 large fresh mushrooms, cleaned, stemmed and halved

½ pound large sea scallops (1½ to 2 inches in diameter)

2 teaspoons flour

2 tablespoons vegetable oil

2 tablespoons chilled garlic butter*

2 tablespoons fresh lemon juice, strained

1 sprig fresh parsley, minced

Garlic butter

6 cloves garlic, peeled

2 shallots, peeled

6 sprigs fresh parsley, washed and stems removed

¼ teaspoon salt or to taste
Freshly ground black pepper to taste

8 tablespoons unsalted butter (divided)

1 tablespoon cognac (optional)

A favorite of dear friends, Dick and Ruth Seeley-Scheel, this dish originated in the now defunct Jean-Paul Restaurant Francais in downtown Milwaukee. It is replete with warm memories for my friends whose adult children have prepared this as a part of a wedding anniversary candlelight dinner for two. It is romantic food at its finest.

Melt 1 teaspoon butter in 9-inch skillet; add onion and cook over low heat 2 minutes. Add tomato and thyme; cook over low heat 10 minutes, stirring frequently; set aside.

In separate small skillet, sauté mushrooms in 2 teaspoons butter over medium heat about 3 minutes until evenly browned. They should retain some crispness. Pour tomato mixture into smaller skillet with mushrooms.

*To make garlic butter pulse garlic, shallots, parsley, salt and pepper in food processor a few seconds, until well-chopped. Gradually add butter, then cognac, if desired. Scrape into small bowl. Cover; refrigerate. Makes ½ to ¾ cup.

Drain liquid from scallops, discarding liquid. Pat scallops dry with paper towels. Dredge lightly in flour. Heat remaining 2 tablespoons unsalted butter and 2 tablespoons oil in a 9-inch skillet. Add scallops and sauté over high heat 1 minute on each side, or until lightly browned. Reduce heat to medium-low; sauté about 2 minutes more on each side. Drain off butter and oil and discard. Add tomato mixture and chilled garlic butter to scallops. Stir with fork until butter has melted and scallops are blended with tomato mixture.

Squeeze lemon juice over scallops then sprinkle with parsley. Serve immediately.

Makes 2 servings.

Baked lemon sole

¼ cup vegetable oil
¼ cup fresh lemon juice
1 pound of sole fillets
3 tablespoons dry bread crumbs
3 tablespoons grated Parmesan cheese
½ teaspoon paprika

Sometimes, simple is best. This recipe illustrates the point beautifully. Only six ingredients and a short baking time produce flavorful fish in a healthful format. Even my mother-in-law likes this fish!

In small bowl, combine vegetable oil and lemon juice with whisk; pour into 13-by-9-by-2-inch glass baking dish. Rinse fillets in cold water, pat dry, add them to baking dish and turn fillets over to coat with oil-lemon juice mixture.

Sprinkle fillets evenly with dry bread crumbs, then with grated Parmesan cheese. Dust with paprika. Bake at 350 degrees 15 minutes, or until fish flakes easily with a fork.

Makes 4 servings.

Baked scrod

1 pound fresh scrod fillets
¼ cup unsalted butter or margarine, melted
1½ tablespoons fresh lemon juice
¼ teaspoon salt
¼ teaspoon freshly ground black pepper
¼ teaspoon paprika
¼ teaspoon dried leaf basil, crumbled
⅛ teaspoon garlic powder
1 teaspoon dried parsley or 1 tablespoon fresh parsley, finely minced
⅓ cup dry bread crumbs

*E*asy fish dishes shouldn't be hard to find but easy, tasty ones sometimes can be. This oven-baked, crumb and herb-topped entree satisfies all my family members. You can use scrod (smaller size fresh cod) or regular cod fillets. Boil up ½ of a lemon in thin slices in a small saucepan with 2 cups of water and a few whole cloves while you cook this fish. Even the most finicky sniffers won't complain.

Rinse scrod and drain on paper towels. Cut scrod fillets into serving pieces.

Whisk together butter, lemon juice, salt, pepper, paprika, basil, garlic powder and parsley in small shallow dish. Dip fish into butter mixture to coat. Spread bread crumbs on paper plate and roll buttered fish in crumbs to coat completely.

Spray bottom of 10-by-6-by-1½-inch glass baking dish (or 9-inch-square by 2-inch-deep dish) with vegetable spray. Arrange fish pieces in dish in single layer. Spoon any remaining butter mixture evenly over fish. Bake in preheated 450-degree oven 15 minutes, or until fish flakes easily with fork.

Makes 2 servings.

Pacific salmon with herbs

1 fennel stalk (divided)
2 shallots, minced
⅓ cup chopped fresh
  mushrooms
5 sprigs tarragon (divided)
5 sprigs thyme (divided)
2 tablespoons peanut oil
  (divided)
⅔ cup red or white wine vinegar
  or lemon juice
1 cup red or white wine or dry
  vermouth
2 tablespoons heavy whipping
  cream
¾ cup unsalted butter,
  softened (divided)
  Salt and freshly ground
  black pepper to taste
4 salmon fillets (6 ounces
  each), skin on

*O*ven-roasted salmon is a beautiful dish with its golden brown exterior and crisp texture. An herb-infused butter sauce accompanies the fish. You may use a red wine vinegar and Pinot Noir wine for the butter sauce as author David Pisegna prefers or a white wine vinegar and dry white wine as my recipe suggests. This recipe is only one of the beautiful regional recipes from Pisegna's cookbook.

From Food for All Seasons; Savory Recipes from the Pacific Northwest, *by David Pisegna. Copyright 1990. Reprinted with permission of Chronicle Books.*

Cut off fennel bulb from celerylike ribs and reserve 1 short (4-inch) rib for use in sauce. Reserve fernlike leaves for garnish. Cut fennel bulb in half lengthwise; dice half of bulb into ¼-inch pieces (to make ½ cup) for stuffing fillets; set aside.

In medium-size, heavy, non-aluminum pot, sauté shallots, mushrooms, 1 sprig each of tarragon and thyme, and reserved fennel rib in 1 tablespoon of the peanut oil until shallots are translucent, about 2 minutes. Add vinegar; bring to boil over medium heat and reduce by two-thirds (about 10 minutes).

Add wine and cook, stirring occasionally, until liquid almost completely evaporates and vegetables begin to caramelize, about 20 minutes. Add cream and cook until mixture thickens, about 1 minute.

Remove from heat; strain mixture through fine sieve into bowl, pressing out all liquid and discarding vegetables and herbs. Return sauce to pan; whip in 1 tablespoon of the softened butter. Return pan to very low heat. As butter melts, slowly whip in 7 more tablespoons butter, 1 at a time, until all are melted.

Remove from heat, cover and keep warm while cooking salmon.

Lightly sprinkle flesh side (top) of each salmon fillet with ¼ teaspoon salt and 2 grinds fresh pepper; turn fillets over so skin side is on top. With sharp knife, starting at wide end of each fillet, carefully peel back skin, stopping 1 inch from narrow edge of fillet so skin still is attached. Place 1 tarragon sprig, 1 thyme sprig, 2 tablespoons reserved chopped fennel and 1 tablespoon butter on each fillet, then lay skin over herbs so herbs are sandwiched between skin and fish; pat firmly with hands to flatten.

Heat cast-iron or other heavy oven-proof skillet over medium/high heat until very hot, about 3 minutes. Add remaining 1 tablespoon peanut oil and 4 salmon fillets, skin and herb side up; brown about 5 minutes. Turn fillets over so skin side is down and bake in pre-heated, 400-degree oven until fish is just opaque in center, 5 to 7 minutes.

To serve, remove skin and herbs from salmon. Spoon warm fennel sauce onto 4 heated plates; place salmon on sauce. Serve immediately with fresh fennel leaves, if desired.

Makes 4 servings.

Grilled catfish & Napa cabbage

- 3½ teaspoons fresh chopped ginger root (divided)
- 3 teaspoons fresh chopped garlic (divided)
- 13½ tablespoons teriyaki sauce (divided)*
- 6 tablespoons olive oil
- 6 catfish fillets (10 to 12 ounces each)
- ½ pound butter, softened
- ¼ cup fresh lime juice, strained (juice of 1 lime)
- 1 teaspoon lime zest
- 1½ tablespoons powdered wasabi*
- 1 package (3 ounces) thin Oriental noodles*
- 1 head Napa cabbage
- 4 tablespoons toasted dark sesame oil
- ⅛ teaspoon ground coriander seed

*C*hef Scott McGlinchey has made a name for himself in southwestern Wisconsin with his signature dishes at Heaven City Restaurant in Mukwonago and Club Cha Cha in Milwaukee. Try his Oriental-flavored grilled catfish with Napa cabbage, Oriental noodles and Wasabi butter the next time you cook catfish. It is delightful!

Make a marinade for fish by mixing in small bowl 1 teaspoon of the ginger, 1 teaspoon of the garlic, 6 tablespoons of the teriyaki sauce and olive oil; pour over catfish in shallow glass dish or in heavy, self-sealing plastic bag. Refrigerate at least 4 hours, preferably overnight.

Whip butter in small bowl with electric mixer until lightened, about 1 minute. Beat in 1 teaspoon of the garlic, 1½ teaspoons of the ginger, lime juice and lime zest.

In measuring cup, mix wasabi (horseradish) and 1½ tablespoons of the teriyaki sauce together until blended; incorporate into lime-butter mixture; cover and refrigerate.

Boil noodles according to package instructions, discarding flavor pack; drain; set aside.

Cut bottom several inches off cabbage; cut cabbage in half lengthwise, then into ¼-inch wide strips (Should make about 6 cups cabbage.)

Heat wok or large sauté pan over high heat until very hot. Add sesame oil, heat 10 seconds and add remaining 1 teaspoon ginger, remaining 1 teaspoon garlic and cabbage. Stir-fry about 1 minute, or until cabbage begins to wilt; add coriander and reserved noodles. Toss evenly to coat. Stir in remaining 6 tablespoons teriyaki sauce and stir-fry 1 minute more; cabbage should stay crispy; set aside.

Heat coals in a charcoal grill, adding apple and maple woods* for flavor, if desired.

Grill drained catfish fillets on lightly oiled grill over hot coals, about 4 minutes per side (depending on thickness of fillet), turning once. Fish is done when it is opaque throughout and flakes easily.

Place cabbage on serving plate, top with catfish fillets and put 1 to 2 tablespoons wasabi-lime butter on each fillet, allowing to melt. Leftover butter can be wrapped tightly in heavy foil and frozen for later use. Serve fish immediately.

Makes 6 servings.

*Notes: Kikkoman teriyaki sauce is preferred. Wasabi, a nose-tingling Japanese horseradish, is found at Asian markets. Oriental noodles usually are called ramen and are sold in soup-mix packets. Apple and maple woods are available at garden centers.

Grilled swordfish with corn relish

4 swordfish steaks (7 ounces
each) cut 1-inch thick
¾ cup fresh lemon juice
(divided)
1½ cups olive oil (divided)
1¼ teaspoons salt (divided)
30 grinds fresh black
peppercorns
2 teaspoons cumin (divided)
½ teaspoon cayenne pepper
(divided)
1 bunch cilantro (leaves
separated from stems)
2 cloves garlic, minced
⅔ cup seeded, diced red pepper
(1 medium pepper)
⅔ cup seeded, diced green
pepper (1 medium pepper)
½ cup diced red onion
2½ cups fresh, uncooked corn
kernels (4 medium-size
ears corn)

*A*ward-winning chef and restaurateur, Sandy D'Amato of Sanford Restaurant in Milwaukee shared this marvelous marinated and grilled swordfish recipe during a class at Ecole de Cuisine in Mequon. His corn-and-sweet pepper relish is a perfect taste and texture complement to the dish.

Place swordfish in large, self-sealing plastic bag. In medium bowl, whisk ½ cup of the lemon juice, ½ cup of the olive oil, 1 teaspoon of the salt, 20 grinds of the black pepper, 1½ teaspoons of the cumin and ⅛ teaspoon of the cayenne pepper until blended. Add stems only of cilantro. Pour marinade over swordfish, making sure all fish is coated. Seal bag and refrigerate 4 hours, turning periodically.

Make cilanatro oil by blending cilantro leaves (reserving a few for garnish), garlic, ¾ cup of the olive oil, remaining ¼ teaspoon salt and 10 grinds of pepper. Puree until just bits of cilantro fleck the oil. Pour into squeeze bottle until serving time. Refrigerate.

In 10-inch skillet over moderate heat, sauté peppers and onion in 3 tablespoons olive oil, about 1½ minutes. Add corn, remaining ½ teaspoon cumin and remaining ⅜ teaspoon cayenne pepper; sauté 1 to 2 minutes until crisp-tender. Drain all but 2 tablespoons liquid from relish. Place in bowl; cool 20 minutes. Add remaining ¼ cup lemon juice and remaining 1 tablespoon olive oil. Taste; add more salt and black pepper, if desired.

Cook drained swordfish steaks over hot coals 3 to 4 minutes per side. Turn steaks only once. To test for doneness, insert knife in center of fish; it should be opaque (not translucent) throughout.

Place swordfish steak next to ¼ portion of relish and drizzle cilantro oil over fish. Garnish with cilantro leaves.

Makes 4 servings.

Marinated roast pork

1 tablespoon Dijon-style
  mustard
½ teaspoon salt
¼ teaspoon ground black pepper
¼ teaspoon crumbled, dried
  leaf thyme
  5-pound boneless pork loin
  roast
½ cup plus 2 tablespoons
  tawny port wine (divided)
¼ cup plus 1 tablespoon soy
  sauce (divided)
3 cloves garlic, minced
2 teaspoons ground ginger
10 ounces red currant jelly
2 tablespoons fresh lemon
  juice

Apple-horseradish sauce

4 tart apples, McIntosh
  preferred, peeled, cored,
  quartered (about 1½ pounds)
½ cup water
2 tablespoons fresh lemon
  juice
1 vanilla bean (3 inches long),
  split
1 cinnamon stick
½ cup sugar
3 tablespoons horseradish

Photo on page 116

*P*ork has always been a favorite of mine. This tender, tasty pork roast is outstanding company fare. Don't let the sauce ingredients scare you away—they are stunning together. Keep this in mind for holiday dinners!

From Noteworthy—A Collection of Recipes from Ravinia Festival, *copyright 1984. Reprinted with permission.*

Mix mustard, salt, pepper and thyme and rub over pork loin's outer surfaces. Place in self-sealing plastic bag. Combine ½ cup of the port, ¼ cup of the soy sauce, garlic and ginger. Pour over pork in bag and seal. Refrigerate 8 hours or overnight, turning bag occasionally.

Transfer meat to roasting pan reserving marinade. Insert meat thermometer in middle of roast. Cover loosely with aluminum foil tent; roast at 325 degrees 1 hour. Uncover and roast 1 hour more, or until thermometer registers 155 degrees for medium; 165 degrees well-done. Baste frequently with reserved marinade. (Pork will continue to cook on standing, raising temperature an additional 5 degrees.)

Remove pork from oven. In small saucepan, heat jelly, remaining 2 tablespoons port, 1 tablespoon soy sauce and lemon juice to boiling; boil 5 minutes, stirring constantly. Pour jelly mixture over meat. Let stand 30 minutes, basting with jelly several times.

Remove pork to warm platter. Slice into ½-inch thick cuts. Strain jelly from pan and pour over meat before serving. Accompany with Apple-horseradish sauce.

Makes 8 servings.

To make Apple-horseradish sauce combine sauce ingredients, except horseradish, in medium sauce pan. Cook covered over medium heat about 20 minutes. Remove and discard vanilla bean and cinnamon stick. Mix in horseradish. Cover and chill in refrigerater.

Makes 2 cups.

Herbed pork chops

1 cup extra-virgin olive oil (divided)

²/₃ cup freshly squeezed lemon juice (divided)

6 sprigs fresh rosemary (divided)

6 sprigs fresh thyme (divided)

1 teaspoon salt (divided)

4 pork chops (about 12 ounces each), cut 1 inch thick
Freshly ground white pepper

4 small zucchini, about 5 inches long

2 sweet Vidalia onions

½ pound shiitake mushrooms

2 sweet red bell peppers

2 sweet green bell peppers

Not many cooks realize that thick-cut pork chops make ideal grill choices. The secret to success is to marinate the meat in a lemon and herb infusion and then grill quickly to avoid overcooking. Remember that pork cooked to "medium"—160-degrees—will be slightly pink and have more juice than pork cooked to a higher temperature but will still be safe to eat, according to Robin Kline of the National Pork Producers Council.

In small bowl, whisk ½ cup of the olive oil with ⅓ cup of the lemon juice. Strip leaves off rosemary and thyme. Finely chop herbs, combine and place ⅔ of herbs and ½ teaspoon of the salt in olive oil mixture; stir to blend (marinade will have green tinge).

Place pork chops in heavy, self-sealing plastic bag or in flat dish. Pour marinade over all, turning each pork chop to coat. Top with a generous grinding of pepper. Put in refrigerator and marinate at least 2 hours or overnight; remove pork chops about 30 minutes before grilling.

Make another batch of marinade by combining remaining ½ cup olive oil, remaining ⅓ cup lemon juice, remaining ½ teaspoon salt and remaining ⅓ chopped herbs in small bowl; set aside.

Wash zucchini, split lengthwise. Cut onions in half crosswise. Brush mushrooms to clean. Seed and quarter red and green peppers. Place vegetables in flat pan; pour new batch of marinade over all, turning to coat. Let stand at room temperature 30 minutes. Drain, reserving marinade.

Drain pork chops, reserving marinade in separate bowl from vegetable marinade.

Over medium coals or on medium-setting gas grill, grill pork chops about 6 minutes per side, or until juices run clear. At the point when you turn chops, brush with marinade, then discard any remaining meat marinade. (Marinade should be cooked as thoroughly as meat since marinade will contain bacteria from meat juices.)

To grill vegetables until just tender, start with zucchini, which takes about 12 minutes; turn once and baste frequently with vegetable marinade. After a few minutes, put onions on and grill about 10 minutes, turning once and basting. After a few minutes more, add peppers and mushrooms and cook 8 minutes, turning once and basting.

Remove both pork and vegetables to warm platter. Serve immediately.

Makes 4 servings.

Pork tenderloin sandwich with red-cabbage relish

- 1 pound pork tenderloin
- 1/3 cup low-sodium soy sauce (Kikkoman preferred)
- 1/4 teaspoon minced garlic
- 1/2 teaspoon grated fresh ginger root
- 1 tablespoon instant minced dry onion
- 1/4 cup beer (any kind)
- 2 cups thinly sliced red cabbage
- 3 tablespoons olive oil plus oil for brushing on bread
- 2 tablespoons white wine vinegar
- 1 teaspoon Dijon-style mustard
- 1/4 teaspoon ground black pepper
- 1 loaf (about 22 inches long) French bread, split lengthwise, or 4 small baguettes (6 inches long)
- 2/3 cup low-calorie mayonnaise

Marjo Green, home economist and microwave instructor adapted this recipe for her classes at Waukesha County Technical College. It uses a lovely, lean cut of pork in a flavorful marinade that combines beautifully with its red cabbage relish. This is a hot sandwich to remember.

Slice pork into 1/4-inch-thick medallions and place in flat, 2-quart glass bowl or self-sealing plastic bag. In small bowl, whisk together soy sauce, garlic, ginger root, onion and beer to blend. Reserve 1½ tablespoons and pour remaining marinade over pork. Let stand in refrigerator, covered or sealed, overnight.

Remove meat from marinade. Place meat in flat, 2-quart glass bowl, cover and cook in microwave about 4 minutes on high power; stir meat, then cook 5 minutes more on 30 percent power, or defrost setting. Allow to stand, covered, 5 minutes. (Or stir-fry pork: Preheat 2 tablespoons of vegetable oil in large skillet or wok until oil sizzles when you drop in a bread crumb; add drained meat; stir-fry over high heat 3 to 4 minutes, turning constantly, until browned.)

While meat cooks, make cabbage relish by mixing in medium bowl the cabbage, 3 tablespoons of the olive oil, vinegar, mustard and black pepper, set aside.

Hollow out halves of bread by removing about 1/4 inch of bread from each half. Brush cut sides lightly with olive oil; toast under broiler at highest heat 1 to 2 minutes. Watch carefully so bread does not burn.

In small bowl, mix mayonnaise and reserved 1½ tablespoons marinade; brush on toasted, hollowed-out bread halves; add tenderloin and cabbage. Slice diagonally into about 3-inch-long serving-size pieces.

Makes 6 to 8 servings.

Stuffed beef tenderloin

1 package (10 ounces) frozen chopped spinach, thawed, squeezed dry
2 tablespoons dry red wine
3 ounces sharp Cheddar cheese, grated
¼ cup dark currants
1 large egg
1 clove garlic, minced
  Freshly ground black pepper to taste
  Salt to taste
1 beef tenderloin (3½ to 4 pounds)
4 canned, roasted, whole red bell peppers*
  Olive oil

I've taken classes from Milwaukee cooking school instructor, Karen Maihofer, for years and always come away with great recipes and serving suggestions. This beautiful red and green stuffed beef tenderloin is probably one of the most popular recipes I've published. It is perfect for the holidays.*

In medium-sized mixing bowl, combine spinach, wine, cheese, currants, egg, garlic, black pepper and salt; mix with spoon to blend ingredients.

Remove silver skin from tenderloin, butterfly-meat, then trim off and discard tail end. Flatten out with meat mallet or the flat surface of a heavy chef's knife to a generous ⅜-inch thickness. Transfer tenderloin to 15-by-10-by-1-inch jelly roll pan lightly greased with olive oil.

Cut peppers into 2-inch lengthwise strips. Place ½ of pepper strips over length of tenderloin, keeping threm 1½ inches from outer edges. Cover with spinach filling. Lay remaining pepper strips over filling.

Beginning at long end, carefully roll up tenderloin and tie with string at 1- to 2-inch intervals. Rub olive oil over surface of meat; season with additional salt and pepper, if desired. If meat has been refrigerated and is not at room temperature, let stand 30 minutes before putting in oven. Roast at 400 degrees 35 to 40 minutes, or until meat thermometer inserted in center reads 135 degrees.

Remove from oven; let stand 15 minutes before slicing if serving hot. If serving cold, let stand 45 minutes, then wrap in plastic wrap and chill at least 6 hours but not more than 24 hours. Remove from refrigerator, slice very thin and serve with French bread or mini-croissants.

Makes 8 to 10 servings.

*Note: Sweet roasted red peppers can be found at Italian specialty markets.

Photo on page 45

Bunkhouse steak salad

1¼ pounds boneless top-sirloin steak, cut 1 inch thick
⅔ cup vegetable oil
¼ cup fresh lemon juice, strained
¼ cup chili sauce
2 teaspoons Worcestershire sauce
½ teaspoon salt
2 tablespoons red wine vinegar
¼ teaspoon crushed red pepper
2 cloves garlic, minced
1 tablespoon blue cheese, crumbled
1 teaspoon seasoned salt*
6 cups bite-size pieces of escarole or leaf lettuce that has been washed, drained and chilled
½ cup cauliflowerets
1 small red onion, peeled and thinly sliced crosswise
1 large tomato, cut in wedges
½ cup canned black beans, rinsed and drained
8 ears pickled baby corn

*P*helles Friedenauer of Rockford walked off with top honors in the 1991 Illinois Beef Cook-Off with this sparkling main dish salad that is as pretty as it is delicious. Beef eaters will love it; calorie counters will find it a perfect compromise in its rich assortment of colorful vegetables. This is perfect for warm weather entertaining.

Trim excess fat from beef and place in shallow dish; set aside. In pint jar, mix oil, lemon juice, chili sauce, Worcestershire sauce, regular salt, vinegar, red pepper and garlic; seal and shake well. Pour ¼ cup of the dressing over steak, turning to coat both sides. Marinate steak 1 hour at room temperature or in refrigerator for up to 8 hours. Add blue cheese to remaining dressing in jar; chill.

After steak has marinated, drain off any excess marinade. Sprinkle both sides of steak with seasoned salt. Broil steak, 4 inches from hot coals or from highest heat in oven, 3 to 4 minutes on each side. Center will still be pink. Let stand 15 minutes on cutting surface, then slice into ⅛-inch strips across the grain.

Cover surface of large platter with escarole. Arrange cauliflowerets, onion slices, tomato wedges and beans over lettuce. Top with steak strips and baby corn. Shake reserved dressing well; pour over all. Serve immediately.

Makes 4 servings.

*Note: I prefer Lawry's brand of seasoned salt because it has no monosodium glutamate.

Savory pot roast

1 tablespoon vegetable oil
Beef chuck roast (4 to
5 pounds)
1 tablespoon seasoned salt
1 large rib celery
1 large carrot, peeled
1½ cups sliced onion
1 can (14½ ounces) chunky
stewed tomatoes with Italian
spices*
¼ cup red wine vinegar
1 small bay leaf
½ teaspoon dried leaf thyme,
crumbled, or 1½ teaspoons
fresh minced thyme
¼ cup water
2 tablespoons flour
1 teaspoon Worcestershire
sauce

*M*eat and potatoes fans, take heart. We haven't forgotten you. This wonderfully aromatic, Sunday afternoon pot roast from my sister Alice Sunseri of Minneapolis wins awards for its flavor and ease of preparation. If you like additional vegetables, team this with Oven-Roasted Vegetables (recipe on page 69.)

Heat oil until hot over medium-high heat in cast-iron skillet or Dutch oven. Pat meat dry with paper towel; place in skillet and brown meat well on both sides, about 3 minutes each side. Remove skillet from heat; pour off and discard fat.

Sprinkle both sides of meat with seasoned salt.

Diagonally slice celery and carrot into 1-inch lengths, to make 1 cup of each. Add celery, carrot, onions, tomatoes with juice, vinegar, bay leaf and thyme to skillet. Cover tightly and roast at 350 degrees 2½ to 3 hours, or until meat is fork-tender. Check every 45 minutes; add water as necessary.

Remove meat and vegetables from pan to heated serving platter, reserving juices in pan. Blend water, flour and Worcestershire sauce in small bowl with whisk. Stir into reserved pan juices. Stir constantly over medium heat until mixture thickens; remove bay leaf. Pour over meat and vegetables.

Makes 6 to 8 servings.

*Note: You can use regular canned tomatoes.

Beef pasty pie

Pastry for 2-crust pie*
5 to 6 medium potatoes, peeled, halved and sliced ⅛ inch thick to make about 5 cups (divided)
1½ pounds coarsely ground lean beef (divided)
1 large onion, halved and thinly sliced to make about 1 cup (divided)
4 to 5 large carrots, peeled and coarsely grated to make about 2 cups (divided)
2 teaspoons salt (divided) or to taste
1 teaspoon freshly ground black pepper (divided)
½ teaspoon freshly minced garlic (optional)
2 tablespoons beef broth or bouillon
1 egg, beaten

*F*aculty member, Bob Rouleau, of Waukesha's Catholic Memorial High School shares a Midwestern favorite. His beef pasty pie is his mother's interpretation of a Cornish classic, the pasty, and can be traced to his father's Upper Michigan roots. Readily available ingredients make this even more appealing.

Line bottom of 10-inch pie pan with 1 pastry crust. Spread evenly onto crust 2 cups of the sliced potatoes, then top with half of ground beef, half of sliced onion and half of grated carrot. Sprinkle over all 1 teaspoon salt, ½ teaspoon pepper and minced garlic, if desired. Repeat layers with 2 more cups of potatoes plus remaining beef, onion, carrot, salt and pepper. Top with remaining 1 cup sliced potato, mounding potato slightly higher in center than on sides. Press down on filling to compress.

Pour beef broth evenly over filling. Place remaining pastry crust over top of pie, sealing edges with water. Press 2 pastry layers together, trimming off excess pastry overhang. Flute edges of pastry or press down with fork. Cut steam vents in top of pastry. Brush top of crust evenly with beaten egg.

Bake on ungreased, 12-inch-round pizza pan in center of preheated, 350-degree oven 90 minutes, or until vegetables are fork-tender and crust is golden.

Makes 8 servings.

*Note: Use your favorite recipe to make pastry or refrigerated Pillsbury pie crusts.

Marinated venison stir-fry

1 pound venison round steak, cut 1-inch thick
½ cup dry red wine
2 tablespoons soy sauce
¼ cup Hoisin sauce
1½ teaspoons chili paste with garlic
¼ cup vegetable oil
2 cups fresh broccoli florets
1 sweet red or green bell pepper, sliced in ¼-inch-wide strips
2 cloves garlic, minced
1 tablespoon cornstarch
4 to 6 cups cooked long-grain rice

My brother, John Hinde, keeps his family well-supplied with venison. His wife, Lisa, supplies that other important part of the game hunter's equation—a repertoire of tasty recipes. This colorful stir fry makes a nice addition to a cook's file.

Cut round steak in 1-inch-long by ¼-inch-wide strips; set aside.

In small bowl mix wine, soy sauce, Hoisin sauce and chili paste with whisk to make marinade. Place steak strips in heavy plastic bag; pour marinade over meat. Seal and refrigerate at least 2 hours or overnight. Then drain marinade from meat and reserve marinade.

Pat meat strips with paper towel and remove excess marinade. Heat oil in wok or large skillet until hot, about 375 degrees. Divide meat into 4 batches and stir-fry 1 batch at a time in hot oil until meat is browned, 2 to 3 minutes per batch. Remove meat to warmed dish; set aside.

Stir-fry broccoli in hot oil (adding more oil if needed) until tender-crisp, about 3 minutes; remove to warm dish. Stir-fry pepper strips with minced garlic 3 minutes; return broccoli and meat to wok.

In small bowl, whisk reserved marinade with cornstarch until blended. Pour over meat and vegetables, stirring to blend. Cook until thickened, about 1 minute. Remove to heated dish and serve over hot cooked rice.

Makes 4 servings.

Rack of lamb with shiitake mushroom sauce

2 racks of lamb, (about 1½
  pounds each, or 7 to 8 ribs
  each), Frenched*
1 clove garlic, peeled
2 tablespoons olive oil
1 tablespoon finely chopped
  fresh ginger root
1 teaspoon chopped fresh
  rosemary leaves
3 ounces shiitake mushrooms,
  cleaned
4 ounces fresh button
  mushrooms, cleaned
1 tablespoon vegetable oil
4 cups prepared beef stock or
  broth
¾ cup Madeira wine or sherry
4 teaspoons cornstarch
4 teaspoons cold water
  Salt(optional)
  Freshly ground black pepper
  (optional)

Julia Child sat across the table from me the first time I ever tasted this incredible dish. It was a luncheon for the International Association of Culinary Professionals' annual conference in Vancouver and the dish was developed by author and cooking teacher Eileen Dwillies. If you love rack of lamb, this dish is for you. Clean your oven after cooking, not before because the high oven temperature causes a lot of splattered fat.

Remove and discard excess fat on racks of lamb, but leave ¹⁄₁₆ inch of fat to cover ribs. Thinly slice garlic into slivers, then rub slivers over loin sections of lamb; reserve garlic slivers.

Stand the 2 racks of lamb up in roasting pan in 2 parallel rows, with meat facing out. Intertwine vertically aligned ribs (as you would your fingers in the "here is the church, here is the steeple" child's poem) and tie rib sections together loosely with kitchen string or unwaxed dental floss.

In small bowl, mix olive oil, ginger root and rosemary; spread over meat with small brush. Sprinkle garlic slivers over meat.

Roast, uncovered, in preheated, 500-degree oven 10 minutes. Remove pan from oven. Remove fat from pan using a stainless steel baster (a plastic baster will melt, as I discovered); discard fat. Or absorb fat with thick piece of absorbent paper towel. Return pan to oven and roast another 6 to 10 minutes, or until instant-read meat thermometer placed in center of meat between the ribs (not in contact with bone) registers 125 degrees (rosy rare). Remove from oven, let rest 5 minutes and unstring before carving into individual ribs for serving.

Meanwhile, make mushroom sauce. Remove and discard stems from shiitake and button mushrooms, then slice both types of

Photo on page 117

mushrooms lengthwise into ⅛-inch-thick slices. In large saucepan, heat vegetable oil over medium heat. Add mushrooms and sauté to 2 minutes. Add beef stock; boil over high heat 15 to 20 minutes, until reduced by half.

Transfer carved lamb to warm serving platter and cover loosely with foil.

Add Madeira wine to roasting pan and "deglaze" by scraping up brown bits of meat clinging to bottom of pan. Boil on top of stove to reduce liquid to about ½ cup, about 5 minutes. Strain through fine mesh strainer into mushroom mixture in saucepan.

Dissolve cornstarch in water in small bowl and stir into mushroom mixture. Bring to gentle boil; stir until thickened, about 1 minute. Correct seasoning with salt and freshly ground black pepper, if desired.

Serve sauce on the side with roast rack of lamb.

Makes 6 to 8 servings.

*Note: Frenched refers to removal of excess fat and scrap meat on top edge of ribs. Be sure to have the butcher remove the chine bones (backbone) from the rack for easier carving.

Goose with apricot-currant stuffing

1 goose (8 to 10 pounds), preferably fresh, not frozen
1 lemon, cut in halves
3 teaspoons salt (divided)
2 teaspoons freshly ground pepper (divided)
1 cup dried apricots, chopped in ½-inch pieces plus canned apricot halves for garnish
½ cup dark currants
1 cup hot chicken stock or bouillon
2 tablespoons port or brandy
5 cups mixed toasted whole-wheat and white bread cubes (about 8 slices)
2 tablespoons minced fresh thyme or 2 teaspoons crumbled dried plus thyme sprigs for garnish
¼ cup chopped fresh parsley
4 tablespoons unsalted butter
1 cup chopped celery
1 cup minced onions

Maybe it is because I grew up reading English novels that I associate a roast goose with holiday entertaining. Whatever the reason, I love the dark moist meat of a roast goose with all of its flavorful accompaniments. Try this recipe with its rich fruit stuffing when the occasion calls for something festive.

Remove all visible fat from cavity of goose. Cut off wing tips at second joint or elbow. Rub goose inside and out with lemon halves, squeezing halves to remove all juice. Prick skin with sharp skewer or clean darning needle to aid in rendering of fat. Sprinkle goose outside and inside with 2 teaspoons of the salt and 1½ teaspoons of the pepper. Set goose aside.

In medium-sized bowl, combine dried apricots, currants, chicken stock and wine. Let fruits soak at least 30 minutes to soften.

In large bowl, combine bread cubes, minced thyme, parsley, remaining 1 teaspoon salt and remaining ½ teaspoon pepper; mix to blend.

In 10-inch-diameter skillet, melt butter; add celery and onions. Cook, stirring constantly, until tender, 2 to 3 minutes.

Combine apricot mixture, seasoned bread cubes and sautéed vegetables in large bowl; cool in refrigerator an hour before packing lightly into cleaned, prepared cavity of goose. Put small amount of stuffing in neck cavity and draw skin over cavity. Fasten in place by inserting metal skewer across cavity.

(Some home economists recommend not baking a stuffing inside a bird. If you want to bake the stuffing separately, put it in a greased, 5-quart casserole and bake, covered, about 1 hour. For flavor and moisture, stuff the goose cavity lightly with additional sautéed chopped onion, carrot and celery pieces, then discard vegetables after roasting.)

Using several metal skewers, draw skin across body cavity together and secure. Using a 2-foot-long piece of unwaxed dental floss, lace or truss the metal skewers until cavity is loosely closed. Tie drumstick ends to the bird's tailpiece with the floss. Then crisscross the floss over back and around base of wings; tie.

Place goose, breast side up, on rack in roasting pan. Roast at 350 degrees 2½ hours, or until meat thermometer inserted in center of upper thigh registers 180 degrees. Remove all rendered fat with baster as it accumulates, every 20 to 30 minutes.

(It may be necessary to cover goose with a foil tent to prevent overbrowning. Remove tent foil during last 10 minutes of roasting to give a golden brown color to the bird.)

Remove goose to carving board and let stand 10 minutes before carving. Carve bird and place on heated platter. Remove all stuffing from bird and serve separately. Garnish platter with fresh sprigs of thyme and canned apricot halves.

Makes 6 servings.

Deep-dish Chicago-style pizza

- 1 package (¼ ounce) active dry yeast
- 1 cup warm water (110 to 115 degrees)
- 1 tablespoon sugar plus 1 teaspoon sugar (divided)
- 1¾ teaspoons salt (divided)
- 1½ tablespoons olive oil (divided)
- About 2¾ cups sifted flour
- 1 tablespoon cornmeal
- ¾ pound sweet Italian sausage
- 1 can (28 ounces) plum tomatoes, seeded, well-drained
- 12 ounces grated mozzarella cheese
- 2 teaspoons dried leaf oregano
- 1 teaspoon fennel seed, crushed in mortar and pestle
- ½ cup freshly grated Parmesan cheese

*Y*ou *can compete with any award-winning restaurant pizza if you use this recipe from the Sunday Chicago Tribune. One of my family's favorite Sunday suppers, this deep-dish pizza is a great make-it-together meal. Someone can form and brown the sausage, or grate the cheese, grind the spices or make the dough. This is knife and fork pizza and the thick-crusted edges are terrific spread with flavored olive oil or sweet butter.*

In medium-size bowl, dissolve yeast and 1 teaspoon of the sugar in warm water, stirring with fork; let stand 5 minutes, until small bubbles form on surface. Stir in rest of sugar, 1½ teaspoons of the salt and 1 tablespoon olive oil. Stir in flour, 1 cup at a time, to make a soft dough.

Turn dough out on lightly floured surface. Knead until dough is smooth and elastic, about 3 minutes. Put in greased bowl; cover with clean cloth and let rise in warm place until doubled in bulk, 45 to 60 minutes. Punch down dough. Brush bottom of 14-inch-diameter, 2-inch-deep, round pizza pan with remaining olive oil; sprinkle with cornmeal. Press dough in bottom and up sides of pan. Rim of dough should be ½ inch wide. Let rise about 20 minutes, uncovered.

To make filling, form sausage into ¾-inch balls and brown in non-stick skillet; pour off any grease; drain sausage balls on several layers of paper towels. Drain tomatoes thoroughly by pressing between several layers of paper towels until most of moisture is absorbed. Coarsely chop tomatoes.

To assemble pizza, place mozzarella in dough-lined pizza pan. Arrange sausage and chopped tomatoes on top. Combine oregano, remaining ¼ teaspoon salt and crushed fennel seed and sprinkle over pizza. Top with an even sprinkling of Parmesan cheese. Place pizza in an oven preheated to 500 degrees; immediately reduce heat to 450 degrees. Bake 25 minutes, or until crust and cheese are golden brown. With wide spatula, remove pizza from pan to a cutting surface. Cut in wedges; serve hot.

Makes 8 servings.

Note: For a vegetarian filling instead of sausage, use sliced fresh mushrooms, sweet pepper strips, olives, and eggplant.

Three-cheese calzone

1 pound frozen Italian bread and pizza dough (Rhodes preferred)
1 tablespoon olive oil
4 ounces fresh mushrooms, cleaned and sliced crosswise
½ cup chopped green bell pepper
1 large clove garlic, minced
1 can (2¼ ounces) sliced black olives, drained
4 ounces prosciutto slices, minced
1 teaspoon leaf oregano, crumbled
4 ounces provolone cheese, grated
4 ounces mozzarella, cut in ¼-inch cubes
¼ cup freshly grated Parmesan or Romano cheese
¼ teaspoon freshly ground black pepper
1 large egg, beaten
1 tablespoon water
2 tablespoons yellow cornmeal

*S*picy Italian turnovers filled with colorful ingredients like green bell pepper, black olives, prosciutto and a mixture of cheeses makes this portable feast an excellent take-along food. These can be made-ahead and frozen and then baked and carried hot to a picnic. Or they may be baked, cooled and then reheated over gentle coals before eating.

Thaw frozen bread dough, loosely covered with plastic wrap, until warm and pliable, 4 to 5 hours. Divide dough into 6 pieces, shaping each into 2½-inch-diameter ball. Let rest 10 minutes for easier rolling. On lightly floured surface, flatten each ball into 4-inch round, then roll each round into 8-inch circle and cover with clean towel.

Make filling by heating olive oil in 9-inch-diameter skillet over medium-high heat. Sauté mushrooms, pepper and garlic until all are soft, about 3 minutes; let cool.

When cool, gently combine vegetables in large mixing bowl with olives, prosciutto, oregano, cheeses and pepper. Spread about ⅔ cup filling on lower half of each dough circle, leaving a 1-inch border around edges.

Whisk egg and water together in small bowl to make an egg wash. Brush edges of each circle then fold over to make a half-circle. Seal edges tightly with tines of fork after dusting tines lightly with flour.

Sprinkle cornmeal over 2 baking sheets. Prick tops of each calzone to make steam vents; brush tops with egg wash. Bake in preheated, 475-degree oven about 15 minutes, or until calzones are crisp and brown. Serve hot. (Bake frozen calzones 40 minutes at 350 degrees brushing with egg wash before baking.)

Makes 6 calzones.

Recipe on page 128 **Oven's apple bars**

Recipe on page 120 **Wisconsin Whoppers** 115

Stuffed chicken breasts   Recipe on page 82

Marinated roast pork   Recipe on page 99

Recipe on page 80   **Chicken with 40 cloves of garlic**

Recipe on page 108   **Rack of lamb with shiitake mushroom sauce**   117

Pepper-Parmesan dressing *(top left)*   Recipe on page 48

Cucumber-dill dressing *(top right)*   Recipe on page 49

Sweet-fruit dressing *(bottom center)*   Recipe on page 50

The Sunday Cook
C·O·L·L·E·C·T·I·O·N

■ <u>Desserts</u>

Wisconsin whoppers

⅔ cup unsalted butter
1¼ cups light brown sugar
¾ cup granulated sugar
3 large eggs
1½ cups chunky-style peanut butter
6 cups old-fashioned oats
2 teaspoons baking soda
1½ cups diced dried apricots or craisins (dried cranberries)
4 squares (1 ounce each) semisweet chocolate
1 package (6 ounces) semisweet chocolate chips
½ teaspoon vanilla extract

A two-fisted high-energy cookie designed for hiking, skiing and all manner of outdoor exercise. Made with lots of old-fashioned oats, peanut butter, apricot bits and chocolate chips, this is a cookie for cookie-lovers. I like to use Jif© brand of peanut butter for best results. These are flourless cookies.

Soften butter on paper plate in microwave on defrost or 30 percent power for 30 seconds.

With heavy-duty mixer, cream butter in large mixing bowl until light-colored, about 1 minute. Gradually beat in brown sugar and granulated sugar; scrape down sides of bowl. Cream until light and fluffy, about 3 minutes.

Beat in eggs, 1 at a time; beat 1 minute more after final addition. Add peanut butter; beat until blended, 1 minute. Add oats and baking soda, beating only until blended, about 30 seconds; set aside.

Dice apricots by hand with sharp knife or process in bowl of food processor using Off/Pulse button until diced in ¼-inch pieces. (If using craisins, add whole to cookies.) Add to creamed mixture.

Cut squares of chocolate in half with sharp knife. Process in food processor until finely chopped, about 1 minute. Blend into cookie mixture. Add chocolate chips and vanilla.

Using a ¼-cup metal measuring cup or a number-20 stainless-steel scoop, fill with cookie dough, pressing lightly into cup or scoop; tap edge of cup to release dough onto lightly-greased baking sheets. Flatten cookies to 3 inches in diameter with bottom of glass tumbler that is dipped frequently in water. Place cookies 2 inches apart. Bake at 350 degrees about 15 minutes. Remove to cool on wire rack.

Makes about 24 cookies.

Photo on page 115

Soft molasses cookie

½ cup unsalted butter,
  softened
½ cup solid vegetable
  shortening*
1½ cups sugar
½ cup dark molasses
2 large eggs, lightly beaten
4 cups flour
½ teaspoon salt
2¼ teaspoons baking soda
2¼ teaspoons ground ginger
1½ teaspoons ground cloves
1½ teaspoons ground cinnamon
  Sugar for dipping

Molasses cookie memories seem to come with childhood recollections. My mother baked molasses cookies; my college house mother baked them, too and when I became a mother, my molasses cookie genes just kicked in naturally. This is the best recipe I have ever tasted in the genre. It comes from a cookbook, The Taste of the Country, Volume III.†

†*From* The Taste of The Country, Volume III. *Reprinted with permission of Reiman Publications, Greendale.*

In large mixing bowl, cream butter and shortening until well-mixed, 1 to 2 minutes. Add sugar and beat until light-colored and fluffy, about 3 minutes. Beat in molasses and eggs until smooth; set aside.

In another large mixing bowl, whisk together flour, salt, baking soda, ginger, cloves and cinnamon. Gradually mix dry ingredients into creamed mixture until dough is blended and smooth.

Roll dough into 1½-inch-diameter balls. Dip tops in sugar. Place 2½ inches apart on greased cookie sheets. Bake in preheated 350-degree oven about 11 minutes. Do not over-bake or cookies will lose their chewy interior. Remove from sheets to wire rack to cool completely. Store in tightly covered container.

Makes about 4 dozen cookies.

*Note: I prefer Crisco. (Don't use margarine.)

Salted peanut crunchies

½ cup butter
½ cup solid vegetable
  shortening
1 cup chunk-style peanut
  butter
1 cup granulated sugar
1 cup brown sugar
2 large eggs, room temperature
2 cups sifted flour
1 teaspoon baking soda
½ teaspoon salt
1 cup semisweet chocolate
  morsels
1 cup salted peanuts

These tiny drop cookies shared by former co-worker, Rita Betlej of Greendale, caused a run on tiny cookie scoops at our local cookware stores. The peanut and chocolate chip-studded cookies are just about perfect, according to column readers. The recipe comes from a vintage Wisconsin Electric Power Company cookbook, no longer in print.

In large mixing bowl with electric mixer, cream together butter, shortening and peanut butter until blended, about 2 minutes. Gradually add sugars, creaming until mixture is light and fluffy, about 4 minutes. Beat in eggs, 1 at a time, beating well after each addition.

Sift together flour, baking soda and salt; mix into creamed mixture until blended. Stir in chocolate morsels and peanuts. Drop 1½ inches apart from a teaspoon or a 25mm cookie scoop onto greased cookie sheets. Bake at 325 degrees about 15 minutes. Remove to cooling rack. When thoroughly cool, store in airtight containers.

Makes about 12 dozen one-inch-diameter cookies.

*Note: Cookie scoops (25mm) can be found at kitchen supply stores.

Wheat germ gems

½ cup butter, room
    temperature
½ cup shortening
1 cup brown sugar
½ cup granulated sugar
2 large eggs
1 teaspoon vanilla
1 teaspoon baking soda
½ teaspoon salt
⅔ cup dry milk powder
1½ cups flour
1 teaspoon cinnamon
1⅔ cups old-fashioned oats
⅓ cup wheat germ
1 cup raisins
¾ cup chopped walnuts

This nutritionally-enhanced drop cookie was a favorite of children and adults alike in the "Moms & Kids in the Kitchen" class I team taught at Waukesha County Technical College. When young children want to help you make something, remember this delicious cookie.

In large bowl with electric mixer, cream together butter, shortening, brown and granulated sugars until fluffy, about 3 minutes. Add eggs and vanilla, beating well to blend.

On separate plate or piece of waxed paper, measure out baking soda, salt, dry milk powder, flour and cinnamon. Add to creamed mixture gradually, using mixer on low speed until well blended. With wooden spoon or rubber scraper, stir in oats, wheat germ, raisins and chopped nuts.

Drop by heaping tablespoonfuls onto greased cookie sheets, about 2 inches apart. Bake in preheated, 350-degree oven 12 to 15 minutes. Remove from cookie sheet with wide spatula to metal cooling racks. Cool completely.

Makes 3 dozen cookies.

Pepparkakor

1 cup unsalted butter*
1½ cups sugar
1 tablespoon dark molasses*
1 large egg
3¼ cups flour
2 teaspoons baking soda
1 tablespoon ground cinnamon
1 tablespoon ground ginger
1 tablespoon ground cloves
1 tablespoon grated orange zest*
¼ cup freshly squeezed orange juice, strained*

*S*wedish spice cookies have been a part of our Christmas tradition since our former neighbor, Norma Herbrand, shared this crunchy, heart-shaped favorite with our family. It travels well, can be used to decorate tiny trees, and is the one cookie that when stored properly, seems to stay fresh forever. Add this classic to your cookie collection.

In large mixing bowl with heavy-duty mixer, cream butter on medium-high speed until soft and light in color, about 2 minutes. Gradually beat in sugar until mixture is light and fluffy, about 3 minutes. Scrape down sides of bowl several times with rubber spatula. Add molasses and egg; beat until well-combined.

In separate large mixing bowl, whisk together flour, soda and spices until blended. Add gradually to butter mixture, beating to combine. Mix in orange zest and juice; blend well, about 1 minute.

On a floured board or surface, roll out one-fourth of dough (that has been dusted with flour) to ¹⁄₁₆-inch thickness. Using heart-shaped cookie cutter, cut dough into hearts; transfer with metal spatula to greased cookie sheets, placing 1 inch apart. Repeat process with three remaining portions of dough. Remaining dough scraps can be worked back into dough portions for additional cuttings.

Bake at 350 degrees until brown, 10 to 12 minutes; watch closely. Remove cookies to wire rack to cool thoroughly. Cover and store.

Makes about 100 cookies in 3-by-2¼-inch heart shapes.

*Notes: Don't use margarine. The small amount of molasses is correct. One medium orange should yield enough zest and juice for this recipe.

Red, white & blue trifle

8 ounces (1 cup) fat-free ricotta cheese

1 package (8 ounces) low-calorie cream cheese, at room temperature

1 cup powdered sugar

1 cup low-calorie dairy sour cream

4 tablespoons hazelnut liqueur or raspberry brandy or 3 tablespoons orange juice*

1 carton (8 ounces) frozen non-dairy topping, thawed*

1 baked angel food cake (about 1½ pounds)

1 quart fresh raspberries, rinsed, drained

1 quart fresh blueberries, rinsed, drained

Keep a patriotic theme in your 4th of July food with this brightly-colored trifle. It is composed of layers of fresh berries, angel food cake and a ricotta-and-cream cheese mixture. You can use non-dairy whipped topping as the recipe suggests or heavy whipping cream, if you prefer. Either way, it is a wonderful dessert for our nation's birthday.

In bowl of food processor fitted with metal blade or in blender, process ricotta cheese until smooth, about 45 seconds. Add cream cheese, sugar, sour cream; process just enough to blend ingredients, about 30 seconds. Pulse in liqueur; set aside.

In deep, chilled, non-plastic bowl, whip non-dairy topping with cold beaters until thick and topping forms spiral patterns on surface, about 3 minutes. Fold in prepared cheese/sour cream mixture with rubber spatula, blending ingredients; set aside.

Brush off golden brown crust from surface of angel food cake and discard. Tear cake into about 1-inch cubes and place in large mixing bowl. Pour cheese mixture over cake cubes, stirring gently to combine.

Place a third of cake mixture in bottom of large glass trifle dish (see photo page 44) or 4-quart glass bowl (glass allows you to see the layers). Place half of well-drained raspberries evenly over cake layer; top with another third of cake mixture. Place all of well-drained blueberries in one layer over top, then top with remaining third of cake mixture. Cover with remaining half of raspberries. Cover trifle dish with plastic wrap. Refrigerate at least 4 hours. Serve chilled in clear glass bowls. Refrigerate any leftovers.

Makes 16 to 20 servings.

*Note: RichWhip, a non-dairy frozen topping, is preferred and is found in the frozen-food sections of supermarkets. Hazelnut liqueur is sold as Frangelico.

Photo on page 44

Summer fruit tarts

2 cups milk
¾ cup sugar (divided)
6 large egg yolks
½ cup flour
1 tablespoon unsalted butter
1 package (17¼ ounces) Pepperidge Farm puff pastry sheets
2½ tablespoons orange-flavored liqueur*
3 ripe nectarines, washed, drained
2 kiwi fruit, peeled
1 cup blueberries, washed, drained
6 ounces apricot preserves
2 tablespoons water

*M*iniature pastries are very much in vogue and Mequon pastry chef, Missie Hawley has developed some delightful recipes for all manner of dainty desserts. These fresh fruit summer tarts with a puff pastry shell, pastry cream filling and bright fruit toppers are sure to steal the dessert scene.

In heavy, medium-size saucepan, scald milk with ½ cup of the sugar by cooking over medium-high heat until small bubbles form around outside edge of saucepan (milk will reach 180 degrees), 4 to 5 minutes.

Meanwhile, in large mixing bowl, whip egg yolks, flour and remaining ¼ cup sugar with electric mixer on medium speed until thick and light-colored, about 3 minutes. Gradually pour scalded milk into yolks, whisking by hand vigorously. Return all of mixture to saucepan and whisk by hand constantly over medium heat until mixture thickens, 3 to 4 minutes. Whisk vigorously and continue to boil gently 1 minute more.

Remove from heat and pour into large bowl. Blend in butter. Cover bowl with plastic wrap on surface to avoid formation of a skin. Refrigerate pastry cream until time to assemble tarts.

Thaw puff pastry sheets (2 sheets about 10 inches square) according to package instructions. On lightly floured board, roll out 1 sheet at a time into a 17-by-13-inch rectangle. Roll corner to corner first, then top to bottom and side to side to achieve a rectangular shape. Lift and move pastry sheets periodically to avoid sticking, adding more flour to board if needed.

Use a 4-inch-diameter cookie cutter to cut 24 pastry rounds from pastry sheets. With 12 of the rounds, use 2½-inch-diameter cookie cutter to cut holes out of center (discard dough centers or bake separately and use in another dessert). With the other 12 rounds, prick surfaces with fork; then, with pastry brush, brush water around outer inch of each round. Carefully place the 12 dough rounds with holes on top of the solid rounds. Lightly tap outer edges together with fingers. Place tart shells 1 to 1½ inches apart on ungreased, 14-by-18-inch baking sheet. Refrigerate, uncovered, 30 minutes.

After chilling, bake tart shells in preheated, 350-degree oven 15 to 20 minutes, until golden. With spatula remove tart shells to wire rack to cool. When cooled, place shells on serving tray; with thumb, press dough centers down in tarts to flatten.

Remove thickened pastry-cream mixture from refrigerator. Whisk in liqueur. Add 1½ tablespoons pastry cream to each cooled tart shell. Refrigerate any leftover pastry cream, covered, for use in other desserts.

Slice nectarines in ¼-inch-thick wedges. Place 2 wedges on top of each tart. Slice kiwi fruit lengthwise into 2 halves; put cut sides down and cut crosswise into ¼-inch-thick slices. Place 2 slices kiwi fruit on top of nectarine slices, leaving room for blueberries in center.

Heat apricot preserves and 2 tablespoons water in small saucepan over medium heat. Whisk to smooth out. When hot, pour through strainer, discarding pulp. Brush hot glaze over fruit on top of tarts, brushing only once for smooth finish.

Refrigerate tarts until serving time. Refrigerate any leftovers.

Makes 12 tarts.

*Notes: Grand Marnier liqueur is preferred. Leftover pastry cream can be used as the base for a larger fruit-filled tart or eaten with fresh fruit slices as a pudding.

Oven's apple bars

2¼ cups flour (divided)
1 cup plus 1 tablespoon granulated sugar (divided)
1¾ teaspoons cinnamon (divided)
1½ teaspoons salt (divided)
1 cup cold unsalted butter, cut into small pieces (divided)
2 tablespoons orange juice or apple cider
1 large egg, lightly beaten
1½ cups sour half-and-half
2 teaspoons vanilla
1 teaspoon lemon juice
4 cups peeled, chopped apples or pitted sour cherries
⅓ cup brown sugar
1 cup chopped walnuts

These lovely, layered fruit bars from cookbook author, Terese Allen, use sour half-and-half as part of their structure. Allen suggests you try pitted sour cherries as well as apples in the fruit layer.

From **The Ovens of Brittany Cookbook,** *Copyright © 1991 by Terese Allen. Published with permission.*

Preheat oven to 350 degrees. Grease bottom and sides of 13-by-9-by-2-inch baking pan (or a 15-by-10-by-1-inch jelly roll pan for a thinner bar).

To make crust, mix together 1½ cups of the flour, ⅓ cup of the granulated sugar, 1½ teaspoons of the cinnamon and ¾ teaspoon salt in large mixing bowl. Cut in ½ cup of the butter pieces with pastry blender (or 2 forks) until mixture is a very fine texture (like cornmeal). Mix in orange juice until well-combined. Pat mixture evenly into bottom of prepared pan. Set aside.

Using an electric mixer on medium speed, combine the egg, sour half-and-half, vanilla, lemon juice, remaining ¾ cup sugar, ¼ cup of the flour and ½ teaspoon of the salt until smooth. Fold in apples and spread over crust. Bake 30 minutes at 350 degrees.

While bars are baking, mix remaining ½ cup flour with brown sugar, remaining ¼ teaspoon cinnamon and remaining ¼ teaspoon salt. Cut in remaining ½ cup butter until butter is size of small peas. Stir in walnuts. Refrigerate topping until batter has baked for 30 minutes. Sprinkle topping evenly over partially baked filling; bake 10 to 15 minutes more. Remove from oven and cool in pan on wire rack at least 45 minutes. Cut in 20 to 30 rectangular bars (depending on pan size). Store bars in covered container in refrigerator.

Makes 20 to 30 bars.

Photo on page 115

Apple pinwheels

2 cups flour
¼ teaspoon salt
1½ teaspoons baking powder
1 cup butter or margarine (divided)
¾ cup half-and-half or evaporated milk
6 Wealthy or Jonathan cooking apples (about 2 pounds)
1¾ cups sugar (divided)
¾ teaspoon ground cinnamon
¼ teaspoon ground nutmeg
1½ cups water
½ teaspoon vanilla extract

Although these apple pinwheels actually look like cinnamon rolls, they are really an easier version of apple dumplings. The sauce cooks into the tender dumplings and thickens as it bakes. Apple dessert lovers—this one is for you!

In medium-sized bowl, mix flour, salt and baking powder with wire whisk. With a pastry blender, cut in ½ cup of the butter until mixture forms coarse crumbs the size of peas. Add half-and-half to mixture, stirring lightly with fork until dough forms ball. On lightly floured surface, roll out dough to 15-by-12-by-⅛-inch-thick rectangle; set aside.

Peel and core apples and cut into eighths (to make about 4 cups); place in bowl of food processor with steel blade and pulse, using ON and OFF switch, until apples are chopped in about ¼-inch pieces. Fold in 4 tablespoons of the sugar, cinnamon and nutmeg.

Spread apple filling evenly over rolled out dough, leaving ½-inch clear around outer edges. Roll up dough, starting at long side; pinch long edge firmly to seal. Using 12-inch piece of dental floss that you slide under the dough roll, cut roll into 12 pieces, each about 1¼ inches wide.

Lift rolls carefully with metal spatula and transfer to a 13-by-9-by-2-inch baking dish, placing in pan with either cut side down. Press dough circles down so that they touch in pan.

In medium saucepan over medium-high heat, bring remaining 1½ cups sugar, water and remaining ½ cup butter to a full boil, about 3 minutes. Remove from heat. Stir in vanilla.

Slowly spoon hot sauce over dumplings in pan. (Don't pour or dumplings may float.) Bake at 350 degrees 1 hour, or until dough is golden brown and sauce is thickened. Serve warm.

Makes 12 servings.

Apple-currant challah pudding

3 tablespoons apple brandy*
½ cup currants
1½ cups unsalted butter (divided)
1½ cups plus 2 tablespoons sugar (divided)
6 medium Granny Smith apples, peeled
1 loaf challah (1 pound), crust removed
½ cup chopped toasted walnuts
2 large eggs plus 1 egg yolk
1 cup milk
2½ cups heavy whipping cream (divided)
¾ teaspoon ground nutmeg (divided)
1½ teaspoons ground cinnamon (divided)
½ teaspoon ground cardamom
½ teaspoon ground cloves
2 tablespoons bourbon

Leave it to award-winning Milwaukee chef, Sandy D'Amato to find a glamorous way to serve what others might term, bread pudding. His fragrant, fruit-topped pudding has apple brandy, challah, spices and toasted walnuts as its foundation. And it is topped with a wonderful bourbon and spice-infused whipped cream. Taste and savor the difference.

Bring brandy to simmer; stir in currants, remove from heat, cover and soak overnight at room temperature; reserve.

To prepare apple layer, melt 1 cup of the butter in an 8-inch-diameter sauté pan over medium-high heat; add 1 cup of the sugar and stir with wooden spoon. Bring to boil over medium-low heat and cook at a gentle boil until sugar caramelizes to an amber color, about 10 minutes. Take care that sugar does not burn. Do not stir but move pan to distribute caramel. To prevent crystallization, brush down sides of pan with water-moistened pastry brush. Carefully pour hot caramel into bottom of 10-inch-diameter-by-2-inch-deep cake pan.

Core apples and cut into quarters; set apple crescents in caramel in a tight circle around outside edge of cake pan, then make another circle in center so that bottom of pan is covered. Place cake pan on a cookie sheet. Bake apples at 400 degrees, 20 minutes. Remove pan to cooling rack.

Slice a square loaf of challah, then cut each slice into four triangles; melt ½ cup of the butter and brush onto each side of the triangles. Toast on cookie sheet in oven at 400 degrees about 7 minutes, until golden. Place half of challah triangles over apples in cake pan, filling in gaps. Sprinkle brandied currants and toasted walnuts over all. Arrange remaining half of challah over top.

Mix together ½ cup of the sugar, 2 whole eggs plus egg yolk, milk, 1 cup of the whipping cream, ¼ teaspoon of the nutmeg and ½ teaspoon of the cinnamon. Pour evenly over challah triangles. Place pan inside a 12-inch-diameter pan, then pour warm water into larger pan until water comes up sides of smaller pan. Bake at 400 degrees 30 minutes. Remove from oven and lift out smaller pan.

Place a 10-inch-diameter piece of cardboard (or bottom of springform pan) over top of warm pudding in cake pan. Place round serving tray over cardboard; invert. Tap top of cake pan and slowly unmold. Any apples remaining in pan can be hand placed on top of pudding.

In a chilled deep ceramic or copper bowl (not plastic), whip remaining 1½ cups of the whipping cream with remaining 2 tablespoons of the sugar, remaining teaspoon cinnamon, remaining ½ teaspoon nutmeg, cardamom and cloves. When mixture reaches soft peaks, in 1 to 2 minutes, add bourbon; whip until stiff peaks form, another 1 to 2 minutes.

Serve pudding warm with spiced cream on the side for garnish. Makes 8 to 10 servings.

*Note: Laird's Applejack Brandy is preferred because D'Amato says it has the most apple taste, but Calvados apple brandy can be used or even regular brandy or bourbon.

Peaches 'n' cream pie

- 1 unbaked pie crust (10-inch diameter)*
- 2 pounds fresh peaches
- 1 cup granulated sugar (divided)
- 5 to 6 tablespoons flour (divided)
- 1 large egg, beaten
- ¼ teaspoon salt
- ½ teaspoon vanilla
- 1 cup dairy sour cream or plain yogurt or vanilla-flavored yogurt
- 3 tablespoons brown sugar
- ¼ cup old-fashioned rolled oats
- 3 tablespoons unsalted butter
- ¾ teaspoon ground cinnamon
- ¼ teaspoon ground nutmeg

A prize-worthy pie recipe shared by former boss, publisher Roy Reiman of Greendale. When I told Roy my husband's favorite pie was "peach" he bet me that his recipe was better than mine. He was right. This has become our peach season favorite and a recipe I've passed along to other peach pie lovers.

Line 10-inch-diameter glass pie pan with crust, trimming and fluting edges as desired. Do not prick pie shell. Chill in freezer or refrigerator while preparing filling.

Peel peaches by plunging into boiling water in large saucepan 20 to 30 seconds, or till skins begin to loosen easily when touched. Immediately plunge into ice water. Slip off skins and slice peaches in half, discarding pits and skins. Slice peach halves into ⅛-inch slices (makes about 4 cups).

Place sliced peaches in large mixing bowl; sprinkle with ¼ cup of the granulated sugar; set aside.

In medium bowl whisk remaining ¾ cup of the granulated sugar, 2 tablespoons of the flour, beaten egg, salt and vanilla, whisking until smooth. Fold in sour cream very gently.

If you use yogurt instead of sour cream, increase flour to 3 tablespoons in this step. Also, you may need to increase total baking time 5 to 10 minutes, until filling is set.

Pour cream mixture over peaches; stir gently to blend. Pour peach filling into crust. You may want to decorate the center of the pie with a pinwheel of peach slices. Bake pie at 400 degrees 15 minutes; reduce temperature to 325 degrees; bake 30 minutes more.

While pie bakes, prepare topping by mixing together in small bowl brown sugar, remaining 3 tablespoons flour, oats, butter, cinnamon and nutmeg. Remove pie from oven; sprinkle topping over pie, leaving a 2- to 3-inch circle in center so peach filling can peek through.

Increase oven temperature to 375 degrees; return pie to oven and bake about 10 minutes more, or until peaches are fork-tender and filling is set. Cool on wire rack. Pie is best served slightly warm. Refrigerate any leftovers.

Makes 8 servings.

*Note: If you use a commercially made pie crust, buy the refrigerated kind by Pillsbury.

Poached pears in chocolate cups

3 cups dry white wine
1 cup water
  Zest of 1 lemon plus
  4 tablespoons of lemon juice
1 stick cinnamon or
  ½ teaspoon ground
  cinnamon
1 piece of vanilla bean, about
  2 inches long (optional)
¾ cup to 1½ cups sugar,
  depending on taste
6 firm ripe unblemished pears
  (Bartlett or Comice)
2 cups semisweet chocolate
  bits

Caramel sauce

2 egg yolks, beaten
½ cup brown sugar
½ cup granulated sugar
½ cup water
¼ cup butter
1 teaspoon vanilla

Simplicity at its best—perfectly ripened pears poached in a fragrant wine-and-spice mixture fill a thin chocolate cup. Top with a lovely caramel sauce and advise guests to attack the pear in any manner they see fit. (After upright presentation, I usually set the pear on its side for easy cutting and eating.)

Place wine, water, lemon zest, lemon juice, cinnamon, vanilla bean and sugar in 4-quart saucepan. Bring to simmer; simmer 5 minutes, remove from heat.

Meanwhile, core pears from the bottom and peel neatly, leaving stem intact. Drop gently into syrup immediately to prevent discoloration. When all pears are peeled, bring to simmer and simmer gently 8 to 10 minutes, until pears are tender through when pierced with sharp point of a knife; remove pan from heat. Cover pan and leave pears in syrup to absorb flavors for at least 20 minutes or overnight; refrigerate covered pan after first 20 minutes.

To make chocolate cups, use 6 fluted foil cupcake cups 2¼ inches in diameter at bottom. Press out flutings at bottoms of cups between your thumb and forefinger to provide a wide base for bottom of pear.

To melt chocolate in double-boiler pan: Bring about 2 inches water to boil in bottom of double boiler; remove from heat; let cool a few moments, then set top of double boiler over water. Put chocolate pieces in top pan, cover, let set 4 to 5 minutes, then stir. Chocolate should form a shining liquid mass. (If you don't have a double boiler, you can set a small saucepan inside a large one with the water.)

Use back of a teaspoon or small palette knife to spread melted chocolate thickly up sides of cupcake cups and in a thick layer across bottom. Set on a tray or cookie sheet and refrigerate, lightly covered with wax paper, until set, 15 to 20 minutes. If storing overnight in refrigerator or if freezing, put cups on paper plate and stick in plastic bag with zip seal, forcing air out of bag. (If you get more than 6 chocolate cups, freeze extras.)

Combine caramel sauce ingredients in small, heavy saucepan. Cook over medium heat, stirring constantly, until boiling, then continue boiling for a total cooking time of 12 minutes, or until mixture is the consistency of thick, pourable syrup. Cool. Store, covered, in refrigerator.

Makes 1⅓ cups sauce.

Just before serving, carefully peel off foil cup from chocolate. Place each drained whole pear upright in a chocolate cup on a dessert plate about 8 inches in diameter. Spoon about 1 tablespoon caramel sauce over top. Serve immediately with dessert fork for easy eating.

Makes 6 servings.

Plum kuchen

½ cup butter or margarine,
  softened
1 cup sugar (divided)
2 large eggs
¾ teaspoon almond extract
½ teaspoon vanilla extract
1 cup flour
1 teaspoon baking powder
½ teaspoon salt
12 Italian prune plums, washed
  and drained
1 teaspoon cinnamon
¼ teaspoon nutmeg
  Whipped cream or vanilla-
  flavored frozen yogurt
  (optional)

In late summer when the Italian prune plums appear in the produce section, buy a dozen plums and make this gorgeous ruby-hued plum kuchen from my friend, Doris Schaffer, of Hales Corners. Its multiple dough flavorings of almond and vanilla are perfect with the sweet, perfumed plums.

In medium-size mixing bowl, cream butter with ½ cup of the sugar until mixture is light in color and fluffy, 2 to 3 minutes. Beat in eggs, 1 at a time, until mixture is smooth. Add almond and vanilla extracts. Beat well, about 2 minutes. Set aside.

In a small bowl, whisk together flour, baking powder and salt; blend into creamed mixture, beating until all ingredients are combined, about 1 minute. Spoon batter into greased round cake pan 9 inches in diameter and 2 inches deep.

Cut prune plums in half lengthwise, removing and discarding pits. Arrange plum halves, cut-side-down, on top of batter in circular patterns, covering all of the batter.

In small bowl, mix remaining ½ cup sugar with cinnamon and nutmeg; sprinkle evenly over plum-topped cake batter. Bake at 400 degrees 30 minutes. Serve warm or cold with whipped cream or frozen vanilla yogurt, if desired.

Makes 6 servings.

Rhubarb rhapsody

½ cup margarine
1 cup flour, plus 2 tablespoons (divided)
1½ cups sugar (divided)
⅛ teaspoon salt
3 large eggs (separated)
2¼ cups rhubarb, cut in ½-inch pieces (about ¾ pound)
⅓ cup milk
⅛ teaspoon nutmeg (optional)
¼ teaspoon cream of tartar
½ teaspoon vanilla

Pie plant or rhubarb as it is commonly known, is one of the welcome signs of spring. Grown in gardens, along fencelines and next to south-facing garages, rhubarb is a profuse producer. Here is a recipe shared by my godmother, Alvina Gehl of Cascade, Iowa for a three-layer rhubarb dessert. I never tire of this tart-and-sweet creation.

Soften margarine on paper plate in microwave on defrost 1 minute. Place softened margarine in medium bowl, and blend in 1 cup of the flour, 2 tablespoons of the sugar and salt with pastry blender until crumbly. Transfer crumb mixture into 9-inch-square glass baking dish. Press mixture firmly to form crust on bottom of dish. Bake in preheated, 325-degree oven 25 minutes, or until lightly browned. Remove from oven and cool on wire rack.

Meanwhile, make filling by beating egg yolks in small bowl until lightened, about 1 minute; then pour into medium-size saucepan. Mix in 2 tablespoons of the flour, 1 cup of the sugar, rhubarb, milk and nutmeg, if desired; stir to blend. Cook, stirring constantly, over medium heat until thickened and rhubarb is softened, about 8 minutes. Pour hot filling over baked crust.

In a deep, non-plastic bowl, beat egg whites with cream of tartar until foamy, about 2 minutes. Gradually beat in remaining 6 tablespoons sugar until sugar dissolves and egg whites are thick and glossy, about 1½ minutes more. Add vanilla and mix. Spread evenly over top of filling or pipe meringue over filling, using a star tip in a pastry tube. Return to 325-degree oven and bake until golden brown, about 20 minutes. Serve warm. Refrigerate any leftovers.

Makes 9 servings.

Rhubarb custard pie

1 unbaked, 9-inch-diameter
   pastry crust*
4 cups fresh rhubarb, cut in
   ½-inch pieces (1¼ pounds)*
3 large eggs
1 tablespoon flour
⅛ teaspoon salt
1 teaspoon vanilla
2 tablespoons unsalted butter,
   melted
1 cup sugar

*W*hen I visit my mother in early summer, she invariably makes this rosy-topped sugar-crumbed rhubarb pie. It is my favorite and she knows it. I make it for my family using the rhubarb plants she gave me and thus we pass the tradition on—of piemakers and their highly-regarded reputations.

Place prepared crust in bottom of 9-inch pie plate. Flute edges or press onto pie-plate rim with table fork; do not prick crust. Spread cut rhubarb evenly over pie crust; set aside.

In large mixing bowl with electric mixer, beat eggs until light and fluffy, about 1 minute. Add flour, salt, vanilla, butter and sugar; beat well, about 2 minutes. Pour over rhubarb in pie crust.

Bake at 400 degrees 10 minutes; reduce temperature to 350 degrees and bake 50 to 60 minutes more, until filling is golden brown. (Shield pie-crust edges with aluminum foil if crust begins to darken.) Let cool on wire rack to warm temperature. Refrigerate pie if not eaten immediately.

Makes 8 servings.

*Notes: You can use a homemade or commercial ready-to-use, refrigerated crust. Use Canada Red or Valentine rhubarb, which are redder varieties.

Rhubarb cream torte

1¼ cups flour (divided)
½ cup butter or margarine,
room temperature
⅓ cup powdered sugar
⅛ teaspoon salt
1½ cups granulated sugar
2 large eggs, beaten
½ teaspoon baking powder
1 teaspoon vanilla or orange
extract
3½ cups chopped fresh red
rhubarb (about 1 pound)
Ice cream or whipped cream
(optional)

If you aren't a piemaker (and most people aren't) keep this lovely pie-like rhubarb-cream torte recipe handy come May and June. It is a treasured recipe from my former boss, Bev Chappie of Waukesha. The easy pat-in-the-pan crust fits nicely in a springform pan and the filling is as simple as 1-2-3.

In large bowl, combine 1 cup of the flour, butter, powdered sugar and salt; rub together with fingers until ingredients are blended.

Press crust evenly into bottom of a 9-inch-diameter by 2½-inch-deep springform pan. Bake at 375 degrees 15 minutes. While crust bakes, combine granulated sugar, eggs, remaining ¼ cup flour, baking powder and extract. Stir in chopped rhubarb.

Remove crust from oven; pour rhubarb mixture evenly into crust. Return to oven; bake 45 to 50 minutes more. Remove from oven; cool 15 minutes. Run wet, sharp knife between pan and torte, then remove rim of springform pan. Place torte on platter; serve with ice cream or whipped cream, if desired. Refrigerate leftovers.

Makes 8 servings.

Spiced pear slab

2½ cups plus 1 tablespoon flour (divided)
  ½ cup plus 1 tablespoon granulated sugar (divided)
  1 teaspoon salt
  1 package (¼ ounce) active dry yeast
1½ cups unsalted butter at room temperature (divided)
  1 large egg, beaten lightly
  ½ cup plus 4 teaspoons milk at room temperature (divided)
  4 pounds peeled, cored fresh pears (Bosc, Bartlett or D'anjou)
  1 tablespoon fresh lemon juice
  1 teaspoon ground cinnamon
  ¼ teaspoon ground mace
  1 teaspoon lemon zest
1½ cups powdered sugar
  1 teaspoon vanilla extract

Slab apple cake has been around for years but Greenfield resident, Gladys Penne has put a new twist on this beloved favorite. With a recipe for a wonderfully manageable dough, Gladys uses fresh pears, lemon juice and zest, and a mixture of sugar and spices to fill the tender crust. Make this in fall when pears are in abundance.

In large mixing bowl, combine 2½ cups of the flour, 1 tablespoon of the granulated sugar, salt and yeast. Cut in 1 cup of the butter with pastry blender until mixture is texture of cornmeal.

In small bowl, mix egg and ½ cup of the milk; stir into dry ingredients until mixture comes together in rough ball (mixture will be sticky). Brush hands with flour and form dough into ball; divide in half. On lightly floured surface, flatten each half into an 8-by-6-inch rectangle. With floured rolling pin, roll out 1 rectangle even thinner, until dough forms an 16-by-11-inch rectangle (edges do not have to be even); fold rectangle in half and then into quarters. Transfer to center of ungreased, 15-by-10-by-1-inch jelly roll pan. Open up rectangle and center on pan. Cover loosely with waxed paper; set aside.

Cut pears into ¼-inch-thick slices (you should get about 9 cups) and drop into cold water with lemon juice to prevent darkening; drain pears well; pat dry with paper towels. Spread over top of dough in pan.

In small bowl, mix remaining 1 tablespoon flour, remaining ½ cup sugar, cinnamon, mace and lemon zest. Sprinkle evenly over top of pears. Cut 4 tablespoons butter into small pieces and dot over pears. Fold up any uneven dough edges around pears.

Roll out second half of dough into another 16-by-10-inch rectangle; fold in half, then in quarters. Put dough on top of pears in pan, unfold and tuck any extra dough underneath bottom layer of dough.

Bake in preheated, 400-degree oven 15 minutes; reduce temperature to 350 degrees and bake another 25 minutes, or until pears are tender and crust is lightly browned.

While pear slab bakes, make glaze by melting remaining 4 tablespoons butter in small saucepan, remove from heat and add 1½ cups powdered sugar and vanilla. Stir to combine (mixture will be thick). Gradually stir in remaining 4 teaspoons milk until glaze is thin enough to pour.

Cool pear slab in pan on rack. While still hot, pour glaze over top crust, spreading glaze with spatula if necessary to cover. Serve warm or cold.

Makes a 15-by-10-inch pear slab that you can cut into 32 squares.

Orange cake with coconut & cream frosting

1 boxed moist deluxe white
  cake mix (18.25 ounces)*
  Grated zest of 2 large
  oranges, about 3
  tablespoons (divided)
1⅓ cups sugar (divided)
  ¼ teaspoon salt
  4 tablespoons cornstarch
  1 cup fresh orange juice,
  strained
  2 tablespoons unsalted butter
  2 tablespoons fresh lemon
  juice, strained
  ½ pint heavy whipping cream
  2 teaspoons rum
  1 package (7 ounces) fresh
  flaked coconut
  Fresh orange slices for
  garnish
  Fresh mint leaves for garnish

*E*aster always meant my mother baked a bunny cake topped with fluffy white frosty and lots of coconut. I liked the cake and coconut part but thought maybe I needed a grown-up celebratory cake. This orange-flavored cake (that starts with a cake mix) is a nice, spring-like cold dessert that would round out any holiday dinner.

Prepare cake mix (it will call for added liquid and either egg whites or whole eggs, mixed in with electric mixer); fold in 1½ tablespoons of orange zest during last few seconds of mixing. Bake cake according to package directions in two 8- or 9-inch diameter layer cake pans whose bottoms have been lined with wax or parchment paper and whose sides have been greased and floured.

Remove pans to wire cooling racks; let sit 3 minutes before inverting pans to remove cakes; peel off wax paper. Cool layers completely, 1 hour. Place in refrigerator 1 hour, uncovered. With sharp serrated knife, slice each cake layer in half, crosswise, so you end up with 4 round cake layers. Set aside.

Make filling by combining 1 cup of the sugar with salt and cornstarch in small saucepan. Gradually whisk in orange juice; place saucepan over high heat. Bring to a boil, which will take about 4 minutes. Then boil 1 to 2 minutes, until mixture is thick and clear. Remove from heat; stir in butter, remaining 1½ tablespoons orange zest and lemon juice. Refrigerate until cold.

Place 1 cake layer, cut side up, on serving plate; spread one-third of chilled filling on top. Repeat process with remaining cake layers and filling, except, when adding fourth cake layer, place it cut surface down. Refrigerate, uncovered, while making topping.

Whip cream with electric mixer on high in non-plastic, chilled bowl until soft peaks form, about 2 minutes. Add rum and remaining ⅓ cup sugar. Continue to whip until stiff, about 1 minute more; spread over top and sides of cake. Pat coconut all over cake. Garnish with orange slices and mint leaves. Refrigerate, loosely covered, until serving time.*

Makes 12 to 16 servings.

*Notes: I use the Duncan Hines brand. This is NOT a pudding cake mix; look for the words "moist and deluxe" on the cake box. Cake will keep up to two days in the refrigerator, but it's best eaten fresh.

Forgotten lemon torte

4 egg whites
¼ teaspoon cream of tartar
2 cups granulated sugar
  (divided)
2 teaspoons vanilla (divided)
5 large lemons, washed and
  dried (divided)
4 large eggs
½ cup unsalted butter, melted
1 pint gourmet heavy whipping
  cream, well-chilled
2 to 3 tablespoons sifted
  powdered sugar

I combine my favorite meringue with a sweet/tart lemon curd filling and whipping cream to satisfy all of my sweet cravings. Maybe it is my imagination, (or my lemon bias) but I think this dessert is as close to heaven as I'll get on earth. See what you think.

In large mixing bowl, beat egg whites with cream of tartar on medium/high speed with electric mixer until foamy, about 1 minute. With mixer still on medium/high speed gradually beat in 1 cup of the granulated sugar until whites are stiff and glossy, about 3 minutes. Add 1 teaspoon of the vanilla; beat until blended.

Spread meringue in well-buttered, 12-inch-diameter round tart pan that is 1-inch deep and has a removable bottom. Build up a ½-inch-wide, 1-inch-deep rim of meringue around top edge of pan. (You also can make individual meringues by dividing batter into 12 portions and spooning or using a pastry tube to form 2½- to 3-inch-diameter rounds on well-buttered cookie sheet, 2 inches apart.)

Bake in preheated, 300-degree oven 1 hour. (Small, individual tarts will bake in about 55 minutes.) Remove from oven to draft-free area; cool completely, then remove sides of tart pan.

While meringue bakes, make lemon curd by grating zest* from 3 of the lemons to make 3 tablespoons grated zest. Squeeze juice from the 3 lemons to get ¾ cup strained lemon juice. Combine grated zest and remaining 1 cup granulated sugar in bowl of food processor or blender and blend to mix, about 30 seconds; add lemon juice and all 4 eggs; blend until mixed, about 30 seconds. Slowly add melted butter that has cooled slightly while continuing to blend. (Butter must be cooled and added gradually so it doesn't cook eggs.)

Pour mixture into top of double boiler; place over bottom of double boiler containing 1 inch of simmering water. Cook on range over medium/low heat, stirring constantly, until thick, 10 to 12 minutes. Remove top of double boiler from bottom, cover lemon curd with sheet of plastic wrap to prevent skin from forming; cool thoroughly.

In chilled, 2½- to 3-quart deep mixing bowl, whip cream with chilled beaters until soft peaks form, about 3 minutes. Add powdered sugar and remaining 1 teaspoon vanilla. Whip until peaks hold their shape and beater leaves pattern on surface of cream.

Spread half of whipped cream on cooled meringue shell(s); cover with all of lemon curd. Spread remaining whipped cream over top of curd or pipe on with a pastry tube. Refrigerate, covered, at least 12 hours before serving. This dessert is best made a day ahead.

Make lemon-zest strips from remaining 2 lemons (wrap and chill lemons for other uses). Just before serving, garnish torte with ring of lemon-zest strips* placed 2 inches from center of meringue.

Makes 12 servings.

*Note: The zest of the lemon is the shiny, thin outer layer that does not include the pithy underside. To make lemon-zest strips, hold washed, dried lemon firmly, place sharp cutting edge of a zester tightly against lengthwise surface of lemon. Press and pull zester to bottom of lemon, cutting zest in tiny strips. Repeat around entire surface of lemon. Zesters are available at kitchen-supply shops.

Cool lime mousse

1 envelope unflavored gelatin
¾ cup cold water (divided)
5 large egg yolks
¾ cup fresh lime juice plus
  3 tablespoons juice, strained
  (divided)
5 teaspoons grated lime zest
  (divided)
1¾ cups sugar (divided)
2½ cups heavy whipping cream
1 tablespoon cornstarch
2 tablespoons butter
¼ cup dry white wine

Limes are lovely, light and refreshing in flavor. So they naturally work well in an airy mousse that can be made in advance and served with an accompanying sauce.

In small mixing bowl, mix gelatin and ¼ cup cold water; set aside.

In heavy medium saucepan, mix egg yolks, ¾ cup of the lime juice, 3 teaspoons of the lime zest and 1¼ cups of the sugar. Cook over medium-low heat, stirring constantly with wire whisk, until mixture is slightly thickened, about 10 minutes. Remove from heat; stir in softened gelatin until completely dissolved. Chill 30 minutes in refrigerator or over ice water until consistency of unbeaten egg whites.

In chilled, non-plastic large mixing bowl, whip cream with chilled beaters until beaters leave pattern on surface of cream and cream forms soft peaks when beaters are lifted out of bowl, about 3 minutes. With rubber spatula, gently fold one-fourth of whipped cream into lime mixture using a down-across-up-and-over motion until blended. Then gently fold in remaining whipped cream. Pour into 1½- to 2-quart souffle dish. Chill, covered, in refrigerator at least 4 hours to gel.

Meanwhile, make sauce by mixing remaining ½ cup sugar and cornstarch in small saucepan. Whisk in remaining ½ cup water, 3 tablespoons lime juice and 2 teaspoons lime zest; whisk until smooth; whisk in butter. Bring to boil over medium-high heat, stirring constantly, about 4 minutes. Reduce heat and cook until thickened but still pourable, about 30 seconds. Remove from heat. Whisk in wine. Chill about 1 hour.

Cut and serve pie-shaped pieces on plates with several tablespoons of sauce.

Makes 8 servings.

Cranberry sorbet

- 3 cans (12 ounces each) frozen cranberry juice cocktail concentrate
- 1 can (12 ounces) frozen cranberry/apple juice cocktail concentrate
- 1 can (12 ounces) frozen lemonade concentrate
- 1 bottle (24 ounces) sparkling (non-alcoholic) white grape juice
- 1 tablespoon peeled, finely grated ginger root

The Old Rittenhouse Inn in Bayfield is well-known for its outstanding food and presentations. This tangy, tantalizing sorbet was served to us during a Murder Mystery six-course meal that was the highlight of one of our weekend stays at the Inn. It is a creation of Mary Phillips, chef and co-owner of the Inn, at her culinary finest. I never taste this wonderful palate cleanser without remembering Mary and Jerry and their gracious hospitality.

Combine ingredients in large mixing bowl to blend (will yield about 10 cups of liquid); chill until cold. If you have a 4-quart (or larger) ice-cream maker, this can be made in 1 batch; if a smaller ice-cream maker is used, divide mixture and make in batches. Freeze sorbet mixture in ice-cream maker according to manufacturer's directions. Package in freezer-proof plastic containers, seal and freeze at zero degrees or below for firm texture.

Makes 4 quarts.

Cranberry-apple ginger pie

    Pastry for 2-crust pie*
    2 pounds Granny Smith apples
    2 tablespoons lemon juice
 1½ cups fresh or frozen whole
       cranberries (unthawed)
    1 cup plus 1 tablespoon
       granulated sugar (divided)
 1½ tablespoons flour
    5 tablespoons brown sugar
    1 teaspoon ginger
    ¼ teaspoon ground nutmeg
    1 large egg, lightly beaten
       Vanilla ice cream (optional)

*W*isconsin ranks number two in the United States in cranberry production so that makes state cooks especially keen on this bright red berry and all its possibilities. This ruby-tinged fruit filling with a touch of fresh ginger is beautiful—and it tastes as good as it looks.

Use 1 crust to line bottom of 9-inch-diameter pie pan that is 2 inches deep. Set second crust aside, covered.

Peel, core, quarter and slice apples into ⅛-inch-thick slices (makes about 6 cups). Slice into water with 2 tablespoons lemon juice to prevent darkening. When all apples are sliced, drain water and lemon juice. Place apple slices in large mixing bowl with cranberries.

In small bowl, blend 1 cup granulated sugar with flour. Stir in brown sugar, ginger and nutmeg; add all to apple mixture in large bowl, stirring with spatula to mix.

Fill pie shell with apple/cranberry mixture, mounding high in center of pie pan. Moisten rim of bottom pastry with water. Cover pie with remaining pie crust. Seal crusts thoroughly by pressing rim edges with finger tips, fluting if desired. Trim excess crusts with sharp knife.

Cut slits for steam vents in top crust; brush with an egg wash (lightly beaten egg) and sprinkle top with remaining 1 tablespoon granulated sugar. Cover fluted edges of pie with aluminum foil to prevent over-browning.

Bake in preheated, 425-degree oven 1 hour, or until apples are fork tender (as tested through one of steam vents). Cool on rack 30 minutes. Serve warm with vanilla ice cream, if desired.

Makes 8 servings.

*Note: Use your own pastry recipe or Pillsbury refrigerated crusts.

Dad's sour cream-raisin pie

1 cup dark raisins
1½ cups water (divided)
1 cup sugar plus 1 tablespoon
  (divided)
4 tablespoons cornstarch
  (divided)
¼ teaspoon salt (divided)
½ teaspoon ground cinnamon
⅛ teaspoon ground cloves
1 cup cultured sour cream
3 large eggs, separated
½ cup milk
1 baked 9-inch pie shell
⅛ teaspoon cream of tartar
½ teaspoon vanilla extract

My father, Glenn Hinde, is a connoisseur of crusts, specifically pie crusts and their fillings. Married to a pie maker for over 50 years, pie still brings a smile to my father's face. This midwestern country classic is his favorite. This meringue recipe does not weep.

In small saucepan, combine raisins with 1 cup of the water; bring to boil. Cover and remove from heat; let stand to plump.

In heavy-bottomed medium saucepan, combine ⅔ cup of the sugar, 3 tablespoons of the cornstarch, ⅛ teaspoon of the salt, cinnamon and cloves. Stir in sour cream; mix well. Beat in 3 egg yolks and milk. Cook over medium-high heat, stirring constantly with wire whisk, and bring to boil, about 3 minutes. Boil 1 to 2 minutes, or until filling is very thick. Remove from heat; set aside.

Drain raisins, reserving ½ cup liquid; add liquid and raisins to filling, stirring until smooth. Pour filling into cooled pie shell.

In small saucepan, mix remaining 1 tablespoon cornstarch, 2 tablespoons sugar and ½ cup water. Cook over medium heat, stirring constantly, until mixture boils and is thick and clear, about 3 minutes; cool to room temperature.

In non-plastic bowl, beat egg whites and cream of tartar with electric mixer on high until peaks form, about 2 minutes. Continue beating, gradually adding remaining 4⅓ tablespoons sugar. Beat until glossy and smooth-textured, about 3 minutes.

Using beaters from meringue (do not clean them off), beat cornstarch mixture slightly, then add to meringue with vanilla and beat on low until blended. Spread meringue over pie filling, making certain it seals edges.

Bake at 350 degrees about 15 minutes, or until golden brown. Serve slightly warm.

Makes 8 servings.

Craisin-pistachio clusters

1 pound white confectionary
coating (also called white
chocolate)*
1 cup craisins (4 ounces)
1 cup natural (non-dyed)
pistachios, shelled
(8 ounces, unshelled)

*D*ried cranberries (craisins) are a relative newcomer to the dried fruit scene. I love their bright red color and their pleasantly tart flavor. They pair perfectly with white chocolate and natural shelled pistachios in this so-simple Christmas candy. You can experiment with varying amounts of craisins and pistachios.

Bring 1 cup water in bottom pan of double boiler to boil over high heat; remove from heat. Cut confectionary coating into ½-inch pieces and drop in top half of double boiler, then place over hot water in bottom pan. Stir constantly until coating is melted and mixture is smooth. Stir in craisins and pistachios.

Drop fruit mixture from tablespoons onto wax paper or parchment paper-lined trays. Refrigerate until firm, about 1 hour. Package in paper-candy liners in covered container.

Makes 36 clusters.

*Note: White confectionary coating is sold in bulk in supermarket produce departments. I used Ambrosia Empress White Confectionary Coating, but Nestle Premium White also can be used.

Pumpkin-walnut cheesecake

- 1 package (4 ounces) zwieback toast, crushed (to make about 1⅓ cups)
- 8 tablespoons unsalted butter (divided)
- 1 cup granulated sugar (divided)
- 3 packages (8 ounces each) cream cheese, softened
- 1¼ cups light brown sugar (divided)
- 5 large eggs
- 1 can (16 ounces) pumpkin
- 1¼ cups heavy whipping cream (divided)
- 1½ teaspoons cinnamon
- ½ teaspoon nutmeg
- ¼ teaspoon allspice
- ⅛ teaspoon ginger
- ⅛ teaspoon cloves
- 1 cup chopped walnuts or pecans
- ½ teaspoon vanilla

Tradition dies hard in my family where Thanksgiving dessert means Pumpkin Pie and Whipped Cream. Period. This departure from tradition was extremely popular with column readers and many have said it has become their new Thanksgiving dessert. Give it a try!

In small bowl, combine zwieback crumbs, 6 tablespoons of the melted butter and 2 tablespoons of the granulated sugar. Press onto bottom of 10-inch-diameter by 3-inch-deep springform pan. Chill crust in refrigerator while preparing filling.

In large mixing bowl, beat cream cheese with electric mixer on medium speed until fluffy, about 3 minutes. Gradually beat in ¾ cup of the granulated sugar and ¾ cup of the brown sugar. Beat in eggs, 1 at a time. Stir in pumpkin, ¼ cup of the cream, cinnamon, nutmeg, allspice, ginger and cloves. Pour into chilled crust.

Combine remaining ½ cup brown sugar and remaining 2 tablespoons butter with nuts. Sprinkle over top of cheesecake. Bake in preheated, 325-degree oven 1 hour and 40 minutes, or until center tests done with a toothpick. Cool in pan on wire rack about 30 minutes. Use knife to loosen cheesecake from sides of pan. Remove sides of pan. Cover and refrigerate until serving time.

In deep, chilled (non-plastic) bowl, whip remaining 1 cup whipping cream with electric mixer and chilled beaters on medium-high speed about 2 minutes. Add remaining 2 tablespoons granulated sugar and beat until cream forms soft peaks. Gently fold in vanilla with spatula. Serve atop wedges of cheesecake.

Makes 20 servings.

Chocolate truffle raspberry cheesecake

3 ounces toasted almonds, pecans, hazelnuts or macadamia nuts
1 package (9 ounces) chocolate wafer cookies
1⅓ cups plus 3 tablespoons sugar (divided)
⅓ cup unsalted butter, melted
5 packages (8 ounces each) cream cheese,* at room temperature
5 large eggs, room temperature
½ cup (4 ounces) Chambord liqueur
1 cup raspberry preserves with no seeds or fruit pieces, or strain preserves (divided)
1 cup fresh raspberries (optional)
Raspberry puree (optional)

Chocolate ganache

2 tablespoons sugar
4 tablespoons unsalted butter
1 cup heavy whipping cream (gourmet cream preferred)
1 pound quality bittersweet or semisweet chocolate, chopped in small pieces
3 tablespoons Chambord liqueur

*J*ill Prescott, owner of Ecole de Cuisine cooking school in Mequon, shared this fabulous dessert with readers in one of my first columns. I asked her for a "light" dessert. She laughed and responded with this one. "I don't really make "light" desserts," she admitted candidly. "If I have to cut calories, I'd rather offer the best seasonal assortment of fresh fruit available. If I'm having something wonderful, I go for complete decadence—like this cheesecake."

Prepare crust by processing nuts, chocolate wafers and 3 tablespoons of the sugar in large bowl of food processor until finely ground, about 30 seconds. Add melted butter; blend about 15 seconds more. Press crumbs into buttered 9- or 10-inch round springform pan that's 3 inches deep. Use a dry measuring cup (metal) to press crumbs into edges. Press crumbs about ⅔ way up sides of pan. Set aside.

To make filling, in large bowl, cream remaining 1⅓ cups sugar and cream cheese together with electric mixer on low to medium speed until light and fluffy, about 1½ minutes. Add eggs, 1 at a time, beating after each addition on low speed. Add Chambord; mix well. Pour filling into prepared crust and place cheesecake on middle rack of oven. Put a cake pan half filled with water on bottom rack of oven (to help stop cheesecake from splitting).

Bake at 375 degrees 45 minutes, or until done. Outside rim of cake will be sturdy and slightly browned; center will wobble just a bit. Turn off oven. Open oven door about 5 inches. Let cake cool in oven 15 minutes, then remove from oven and place on wire rack to cool. Loosen edges between cake and pan with knife, to prevent cake from splitting.

Cool about 1½ hours. Refrigerate 3 hours to cool completely. Then remove sides from pan by carefully pushing up springform bottom.

Spread about ¾ cup of the raspberry preserves in thin layer on top of cooled cake.

To make ganache, combine sugar, butter and cream in heavy-bottomed, 2-quart saucepan; heat over low heat about 3 minutes, until sugar is dissolved. Place chopped chocolate in medium-size bowl; add hot cream mixture and whip well with wire whisk until chocolate melts and mixture is smooth. Add Chambord; mix.

Place bowl with chocolate in larger bowl filled with ice and cold water. Stir chocolate mixture constantly with spatula, scraping from bottom, until ganache cools and thickens enough to pipe through a pastry bag, 5 to 10 minutes; do not let chocolate harden. Remove from ice water.

Makes about 3 cups.

Using a pastry bag with a star tip, pipe chocolate ganache on outside rim of top of cake. If desired, frost sides of cake with ganache, too. For extra flourish, decorate top of cake with fresh raspberries, if desired; then, using a pastry brush, glaze raspberries with about ¼ cup of raspberry preserves that have been heated over low heat a few minutes until liquid.

Cut cheesecake into small pie-wedge slices while still cold by using a knife dipped in hot water each time you cut. After cheesecake has been cut, leave at room temperature about 30 minutes before serving. Serve plain or put each piece on a small pool of raspberry puree made by pressing thawed, frozen raspberries through a food mill or sieve and sweetening to taste, adding some Chambord if desired.

Makes 10 to 12 servings.

*Notes: Fleur de Lait cream cheese is preferred. It is made without guar gum and available at specialty food stores.

Flourless chocolate cake

12 ounces quality semisweet chocolate
2 ounces unsweetened chocolate
1 cup (2 sticks) unsalted butter
2 tablespoons Grand Marnier liqueur
1 teaspoon vanilla extract
¼ teaspoon almond extract
10 eggs, room temperature (separated)
1½ cups granulated sugar (divided)
Powdered sugar for decoration
Fresh strawberries, if desired

Creme Anglaise

1½ cups milk (2% or whole milk)
1 piece vanilla bean (1 inch long), split open
3 egg yolks
⅓ cup sugar

Restaurant dessert menus often offer their version of flourless chocolate cake which I have found generally to be dense, heavy and brownie-like. My version is lighter and softer and tastes like intense chocolate in airy mouthfuls. Serve it with a pool of Creme Anglaise keeping the servings small. "Less is more" in this delectable dessert.

Heat 1 inch of water in bottom of double boiler over medium-low heat until it simmers. Cut both chocolates into small chunks and place in top of double boiler with butter, liqueur, vanilla and almond extracts; set over simmering water in bottom pan, stirring ingredients until melted, 6 to 7 minutes. Remove top of double boiler from heat. Whip chocolate mixture lightly with whisk, 1 to 2 minutes; set aside.

In large bowl of heavy-duty electric mixer, whip egg yolks on medium-high speed, adding ¾ cup sugar gradually until mixture turns a creamy white and is very thick, 5 to 7 minutes. Gently fold egg-yolk mixture into chocolate mixture with spatula, combining thoroughly. Set aside.

In separate mixing bowl, whip egg whites with electric mixer on medium/high speed until frothy, about 2 minutes. Slowly beat in remaining ¾ cup sugar, whipping until smooth and glossy, 4 to 5 minutes. With spatula, carefully fold about 1 cup egg whites into chocolate mixture to lighten it. With spatula, fold in remaining egg whites, carefully blending in a down-up-and-over folding motion that maintains the lightness of the mixture; set aside.

Butter 2 round 9-by-2-inch cake pans, sprinkle with flour, and line bottom of pans with parchment paper. Carefully pour half of batter into each pan, spreading batter evenly. Bake at 275 degrees 1 hour 20 minutes to 1 hour 25 minutes. Cake consistency should be moist but cakelike, not liquidy.

Loosen edges of cakes with knife or metal spatula and invert pans over cooling racks to remove cakes. Carefully remove parchment paper because cake bottoms will become cake tops; cool thoroughly. A flaky crust will appear on cakes. Simply brush away lightly. Cakes will fall slightly in center when cooled.

To make Creme Anglaise, heat milk and vanilla bean in small saucepan over medium-high heat until milk scalds, 180 degrees, about 6 minutes. Remove pan from heat; cool 10 minutes. Discard vanilla bean.

In small mixing bowl of electric mixer, beat egg yolks with sugar until mixture thickens. Gradually whisk in milk with wire whisk. Place mixture in top of double boiler and sit over gently simmering water in bottom of double boiler; cook custard over medium-low heat, stirring constantly until it thickens, about 15 minutes. (Do not increase temperature or custard may curdle.) Test doneness by dipping a large metal spoon into custard. Run your index finger across mixture on back of the spoon; when it holds the line drawn, the mixture is thick enough. Remove from heat; place top of double boiler over ice water, stirring occasionally until cooled. Store, covered, in refrigerator.

To serve, place on serving plates. Lay a 9-inch paper doily on top of each cake; sift powdered sugar over doily top to make a decorative finish; remove doilies. Garnish with a few fresh, washed, unhulled strawberries. Cut cakes in 12 wedges. Serve on dessert plates that have 1½ tablespoons of creme Anglaise spooned into center.

Makes 24 servings.

Note: If you wish to freeze 1 cake, wrap cake (without powdered sugar topping) tightly in heavy-duty aluminum foil, sealing well. Remove from freezer 2 hours before serving.

Chocolate decadence torte

1 cup sugar
⅓ cup water plus 1½ teaspoons (divided)
1 to 2 tablespoons orange-flavored liqueur
1 baked 8- or 9-inch-diameter-by-1½-inch-high chocolate cake layer, cooled*
9 ounces bittersweet chocolate (Callebaut preferred), finely chopped (divided)
1 cup heavy whipping cream (divided)
2 tablespoons slivered almonds
¼ cup raspberry or strawberry jam
9 teaspoons plain non-fat yogurt, well-blended
2 ounces white chocolate, melted
Fresh mint leaves for garnish
Fresh raspberries for garnish

*I*n the picturesque village of Kohler, guests at The American Club resort are pampered in every conceivable way. Among the pleasures of a stay at this five-diamond AAA rated resort are the glorious food. This exquisite chocolate dessert for two was created by pastry chef, Richard Palm for Wisconsin readers. If you like this dessert, consider reserving a spot at the American Club's annual "In Celebration of Chocolate" each December. It will satisfy your every chocolate craving.

In small saucepan over medium heat bring sugar and water just to a boil, stirring constantly to dissolve sugar. Remove from heat and chill thoroughly (until cold to the touch) in refrigerator. When chilled, add liqueur; set aside.

Using a heart-shaped cookie cutter 4 to 5 inch by 1 inch deep, cut 1 heart from chocolate cake layer. Slice heart cake horizontally with a serrated knife to make 2 thin layers. Brush, but do not soak, top surfaces of cake layers with reserved chilled syrup; refrigerate.

Heat 1 inch of water in bottom of double-boiler pan until simmering. Remove from heat. Place 3 ounces of the chopped chocolate in top of double boiler and set over bottom pan containing very warm water. Stir until completely melted and smooth. Remove top pan and set on rack to cool to 110 degrees.

Meanwhile, in small, deep, chilled metal mixing bowl with chilled beaters, beat ½ cup of chilled whipping cream on high until stiff, about 1½ minutes. Whisk ¼ of cream into melted chocolate, scraping sides of bowl to mix well. Fold remaining ¾ of cream into chocolate mixture until thoroughly blended; refrigerate.

In 2-quart saucepan, bring remaining ½ cup of unwhipped cream to a boil. Remove from heat; add remaining 6 ounces chopped chocolate, whisking until smooth. Chill chocolate glaze until it is the consistency of heavy cream.

Meanwhile, toast almonds on flat pan in oven at 350 degrees 3 to 5 minutes, watching carefully; remove from pan; cool; chop until very fine.

In small saucepan, heat raspberry jam until softened. Strain to remove pulp and seeds. Stir in 1½ teaspoons water until consistency of syrup.

To assemble cake, place 1 heart layer, syrup side up, in center of plate. Top with ⅔ of chocolate whipped cream. Place second heart, syrup side up, on top of cream. Spread remaining whipped cream over second layer. Cover cake loosely with aluminum foil and freeze until firm, at least 2 hours.

Remove heart cake from plate and carefully transfer with wide spatula to wire rack with wax paper underneath to catch drippings. Pour chocolate glaze over top of heart to cover. (If chocolate glaze is too firm to be pourable, soften over pan of warm water, stirring to blend.) With wide spatula, transfer glazed heart to center of decorative dessert plate. Press narrow band of toasted almonds all around base of heart, about ¼ inch high, using back of small spoon to push into glaze.

Pour pool of liquefied raspberry jam around heart. Drop tiny dollops of yogurt in jam, drawing off and curling ends of yogurt in star pattern with a thin bamboo skewer. Do not clean off skewer tips between designs.

Garnish plate with fresh mint leaves and raspberries. Chill until serving time.

Makes 2 generous servings.

*Notes: For convenience, we use a standard 8-or 9-inch cake pan, even though we need only a 4- to 5-inch cake. For the chocolate cake, I recommend using a commercial mix for an extra-moist, double-layer chocolate cake and freezing the leftover layer for future use.

Chocolate hazelnut demise

1⅓ cups whole hazelnuts* plus 16 whole hazelnuts for garnish (divided)
1 cup flour
1⅓ cups plus 2 tablespoons unsweetened cocoa (divided)
1 cup plus 4 teaspoons granulated sugar (divided)
¼ teaspoon salt
1 cup plus 13 tablespoons unsalted butter, softened (divided)
12 ounces cream cheese, softened
15 ounces white chocolate (divided)
3 tablespoons vegetable shortening (divided)
½ cup hazelnut liqueur (divided)*
1 cup semisweet chocolate chips
¼ cup water
¾ cup powdered sugar

*A*t the Inn at Cedar Crossing in downtown Sturgeon Bay, pastry chef Jeanne Demers turns out incredible creations daily to satisfy the sweet cravings of the Inn's clientele. Next to Door County cherry pies, chocolate concoctions are the most popular dessert, according to Demers. She designed this rich dessert especially for Wisconsin *readers.*

Toast hazelnuts on baking sheet in preheated, 350-degree oven until skins split, about 5 minutes. Remove and rub between surfaces of clean towel to remove skins. Discard skins and set 16 hazelnuts aside for garnish; finely grind about 1 cup of remaining hazelnuts in food processor; set aside. Chop remaining ⅓ cup hazelnuts for garnish; set aside.

To make crust, in large mixing bowl blend flour, ⅓ cup of the cocoa, ⅓ cup of the granulated sugar, salt and 7 tablespoons of the butter with pastry blender until crumbly. Press firmly onto bottom of 9-inch-diameter springform pan that has been greased and dusted with flour. Bake at 350 degrees 10 minutes. Cool in refrigerator or freezer.

Make white-chocolate layer by beating cream cheese and 6 tablespoons of the butter with electric mixer until smooth and creamy, about 3 minutes. In small, heavy-bottomed pan over low heat, melt 12 ounces of the white chocolate and 2 tablespoons of the vegetable shortening until smooth; then add to cream-cheese mixture and beat until smooth, about 1 minute. Stir in ¼ cup of the liqueur and ½ cup of the reserved ground hazelnuts. Spread evenly over pre-baked crust. Place in freezer to firm.

Prepare dark-chocolate layer by melting semisweet chocolate chips in small, heavy-bottomed pan over low heat; set aside to cool. In small saucepan over medium heat, bring water and ¾ cup of the granulated sugar to a boil. When sugar is dissolved, set aside to cool.

In large mixing bowl with electric mixer, beat remaining 1 cup plus 2 tablespoons cocoa, remaining 1 cup butter and ¾ cup powdered sugar on medium speed until well-combined, about 2 minutes. Beat in cooled, melted chocolate and cooled sugar syrup. Stir in remaining ¼ cup liqueur and remaining ½ cup ground hazelnuts. Spread over chilled, white-chocolate layer; chill in refrigerator until set, at least 2 hours.

Make decorative topping by melting remaining 3 ounces white chocolate and remaining 1 tablespoon vegetable shortening in small, heavy-bottomed saucepan over low heat; stir until smooth. Using a spoon, drizzle mixture over top of cake in decorative pattern. Place 16 whole hazelnuts equal distances apart around edge to mark individual servings. Sprinkle reserved chopped hazelnuts around top forming a ring just inside the whole nuts. Cut into 16 pieces with a wet, hot knife.

Makes 16 servings.

*Notes: Here is a tip from cooks who made this dessert. Try to buy pre-shelled hazelnuts for easier removal of skins. We used Frangelico hazelnut liqueur. This cheesecake will last up to a week refrigerated.

White-chocolate terrine

- 11½ ounces of white chocolate bar (divided)
- 2½ teaspoons unflavored gelatin
- 10 tablespoons water (divided)
- 3 large egg yolks
- 3 tablespoons white corn syrup (divided)
- 14 ounces heavy whipping cream
- 1¾ teaspoons vanilla extract (divided)
- 1 package (10 ounces) whole frozen raspberries, thawed
- 6 tablespoons sugar (divided)
- 2 ripe mangoes, peeled and seeded
- 3 tablespoons cocoa powder (optional)

*C*hef Steven Wade Klindt continues to dazzle his patrons at his intimate Steven Wade Cafe in New Berlin. Innovative, cutting edge entrees, salads and appetizers characterize his ever-evolving menu. Klindt has distinguished himself with his chocolate dessert creations. This one is a peerless example of his skill and craft.

Finely shred 10 ounces of the chocolate, then melt shreds in top of double boiler (or in medium-size stainless-steel bowl) set over bottom of double boiler holding 1 inch of simmering water. When chocolate is melted, remove from heat, stir until smooth, pour into deep metal bowl and set aside.

Clean out top of double boiler and cool (or use a spare top pan). Add gelatin and 6 tablespoons of the water, mix and let stand a few minutes.

In small bowl, mix egg yolks and 2 tablespoons of the corn syrup well, then add to gelatin in top of double-boiler pan; place over bottom of double boiler filled 1 inch with simmering water. Attach candy thermometer to inside edge of top pan. Using wire whisk or portable mixer on medium speed, whip until mixture reaches full volume and thermometer reads 140 degrees (it will take about 12 minutes). Remove from range but keep pan over heated water 3½ minutes (temperature will stay at 140 degrees, which will heat the egg sufficiently).

Remove top pan from heated water and set aside to cool 2 minutes. Fold egg mixture into reserved melted chocolate in metal bowl; transfer thermometer to inside edge of bowl; cool mixture to 75 degrees (it will become pudding-like and thick).

In large, deep, chilled (non-plastic) mixing bowl with chilled beaters, whip heavy cream and 1½ teaspoons of the vanilla until soft peaks form when beaters are lifted out of mixture, about 2 minutes.

Gently fold ½ cup of the whipped cream into cooled chocolate mixture to lighten it. Add remaining whipped cream, folding in gently.

Using largest holes on a grater, shave remaining 1½ ounces white chocolate. Fold shavings into chocolate-gelatin mixture. Pour into parchment-lined 11-by-4-by-2-inch terrine pan. Gently tap filled pan a few times on firm surface to remove air bubbles. Cover tightly with plastic wrap; refrigerate at least 12 hours (or up to 3 days).

Make raspberry sauce by placing raspberries in food processor or blender. Process until smooth, 1 to 2 minutes; pour puree through a fine mesh strainer. Place ½ of strained puree and ¼ cup sugar in small saucepan. Heat over medium heat until sugar dissolves, about 1½ minutes. Fold heated puree into reserved half of unheated puree. Stir to blend. Cover and refrigerate.

Puree mangoes in food processor until smooth, about 2 minutes. Place puree, remaining 4 tablespoons water, remaining 1 tablespoon corn syrup, remaining 2 tablespoons sugar and remaining ¼ teaspoon vanilla in small saucepan. Over medium-low heat, bring mixture to simmer. Strain heated puree through fine mesh strainer. Refrigerate, covered, until time to use.

To unmold chilled terrine, invert on flat tray. Gently pull off parchment paper. Slice terrine into 12 portions. Place each slice centered on a chilled plate.

Spoon mango sauce on half of plate surrounding terrine; spoon raspberry sauce on other half. Garnish each sauce with raspberries, blackberries or blueberries, depending on availability. Sprinkle a small amount of cocoa powder, if desired, onto each plate rim.

Makes 12 rich servings.

Chocolate-dipped apricots

1 cup semisweet chocolate
  chips (6 ounces)
1 square (1 ounce)
  unsweetened baking
  chocolate, cut into ½-inch
  pieces
60 whole dried apricots
  (1 pound)

No matter where we spend Christmas, these simple, yet elegant treats always make the trip. I've made them in Cancun, Key West and in Aspen, carrying my supplies along in my luggage. The chocolate-apricot combination simply can't be topped.

Line 2 trays with parchment paper or wax paper. Spray lightly with vegetable-oil spray; set aside.

Heat 1 cup water to a boil over high heat in bottom of double boiler; remove from heat. Mix chocolate chips and unsweetened chocolate pieces in top pan of double boiler and set over hot water in bottom pan; stir constantly until chocolate melts.

Dip apricots halfway into chocolate. Shake excess chocolate from apricots into pan. Place dipped apricots on prepared trays. Refrigerate until firm, about 1 hour.

Makes 60 apricots.

Coconut balls

1 cup pitted dried prunes
 (about 8 ounces)
1 cup water
1 cup dried apricots (6 ounces)
1 cup golden raisins
1½ cups pitted dates (about
 12 ounces)
1¼ cups walnuts
2 cups flaked coconut
 (6 ounces)

Only natural sugars sweeten these dried fruit confections that are mixed with walnuts and rolled in coconut. A favorite of my children, Jon and Anne, who still expect to find them among the Christmas sugar plums. Use an old-fashioned crank-style food grinder to process this fruit, if you have one.

In medium saucepan, bring prunes and water to boil; reduce heat to simmer, cover and cook 8 minutes. Drain and discard any liquid from prunes. Let prunes cool 30 minutes.

In food grinder fitted with a coarse blade (or in bowl of food processor), mix cooked prunes, apricots, raisins, dates and walnuts; grind into shallow pan. (Or, using pulse/off button on food processor, pulse until fruits are ground about ¼-inch in size.) Refrigerate at least 2 hours.

With hands, form chilled fruit mixture into 1-inch-diameter balls; then roll balls in coconut (spread on paper plate) until completely covered. Store in tight-fitting covered container in refrigerator.

Makes about 48 fruit balls.

Mom's peanut brittle

2 cups granulated sugar
1 cup white corn syrup
3 cups raw peanuts
3 teaspoons baking soda

*M*y mother, Inez Hinde, has been making this special airy peanut brittle for years and packing it off to her six children every Christmas holiday. Her recipe was a secret, but she decided to share it with Wisconsin readers. Here it is—with Mom's admonition. "Don't flatten out the brittle when you pour it on the baking sheet." That's the secret!

In heavy, 3½-quart saucepan, mix sugar and corn syrup; stir with long-handled wooden spoon until blended. Clip candy thermometer onto side of pan, making sure thermometer bulb is immersed in mixture but not resting on bottom of pan. Cook over medium-high heat, stirring frequently, until syrup reaches soft-ball stage (234 degrees).

Add peanuts (with skins still on) all at once, stirring to blend; reduce heat to medium and cook, stirring frequently, until candy thermometer registers 306 degrees,* six degrees above the hard-crack stage (syrup at 300 degrees forms brittle threads when a bit is drizzled onto wax paper).

Remove from heat. Add baking soda, stirring well to blend. (Mixture will be light and fluffy.) Pour quickly down the length of buttered, 15-by-10-by-1-inch jelly roll pan. Let candy spread out on its own; do NOT spread with a spoon or spatula. Cool completely; break into pieces. Store in an airtight container.

Makes 2½ pounds of brittle.

*Note: Six degrees is represented on a candy thermometer by three graduated marks or three lines.

The Sunday Cook
C·O·L·L·E·C·T·I·O·N

■ Index

■ ■ ■

For additional copies of

THE SUNDAY COOK COLLECTION

or for a copy of

ENCORE WISCONSIN *by Grace Howaniec*

contact:

AMHERST PRESS

318 N. Main St.

Amherst, WI 54406

or Call: 715-824-3214 or Tollfree: 1-800-333-8122

FAX orders to: 715-824-5806